Schools in a Changing Society

Schools
in a
Changing Society

EDITED AND WITH AN INTRODUCTION BY

Albert J. Reiss, Jr.

30656

THE FREE PRESS, NEW YORK
COLLIER-MACMILLAN LIMITED, LONDON

PREFACE

There have been numerous conferences devoted to the problems of schools in a changing society and the reader will want to know in what way this one was intended to differ from others. Whether or not it actually succeeded in doing so is for the reader to decide.

A brief history of the conference may help the reader to answer his question. A review of the literature on schools disclosed that there was very little research on ways that the administrative organization of school systems had consequences for the socialization of youth in the school and in the community. Indeed, it is characteristic of the research literature until very recently that it took the organization of school systems for granted; research problems were formulated without regard to variation in the structural elements or organizational mechanisms of school systems.

Recent attempts to take account of organizational aspects of schools often are not germane since they focus either on the social structure of the classroom or on some aspect of the social composition of the schools, such as its social-class composition. Though such studies *are* of value to the administrators of school systems, it is all too apparent that there is relatively little research on how administrative organization of a school system relates to contemporary problems confronting school administrators and policy makers. Not that the literature on school administration is sparse. Quite the contrary. There is a considerable literature on school administration, but much of it is written by professional administrators on the basis of their experience, and the research studies generally deal with the "classic" problems of internal administration of schools or the characteristics of the administrators and their work roles. Moreover, especially lacking are studies where aspects of the organization of school systems are investigated for their effects on problems of youth and their relationship to the community.

Some effort, therefore, was made to locate investigations currently underway on such problems, particularly as they dealt with factors that might be subject to administrative decision making. A number of studies were located where there not only was a concern with these problems but where the investigators themselves were more or less involved with programs in school systems in which administrators had an active interest. They were, in sum, programs oriented toward changes in organizational aspects of school systems.

A decision then was made to bring these investigators together with administrators who were responsible for the formation of school policy and its implementation. The purpose of the conference was to utilize these studies as a basis for a broad consideration of the kind of research necessary to the formation of enlightened public policy regarding the contemporary problems of schools. The focus, however, was clearly to be on ways that the organizational system might be manipulated for dealing with these problems.

The conference was held at Inglis House, University of Michigan on February 7 and 8, 1964. The papers presented at the conference, and published in this volume, served as a basis for discussion there. The following administrators were invited and participated in the conference:

Carl L. Byerly, Assistant Superintendent, Detroit Public Schools, Detroit, Michigan

William J. Cunningham, Assistant Superintendent, Curriculum Development, School Committee of the City of Boston, Boston, Massachusetts

Carl Hansen, Superintendent, District of Columbia Schools, Washington, D.C.

David A. Horowitz, Associate Superintendent, School District of Philadelphia, Board of Public Education, Philadelphia, Pennsylvania

Irene C. Hypps, Assistant Superintendent, Public Schools of the District of Columbia, Washington, D.C.

Lawrence L. Jarvie, General Superintendent, Flint Board of Education, Flint, Michigan

Jacob Landers, Assistant Superintendent, Board of Education of the City of New York, Brooklyn, New York

Carl L. Marburger, Director, Greater Cities School Improvement Project, Detroit, Michigan

Blanche B. Paulson, Director, Bureau of Pupil Personnel Services, Board of Education of the City of Chicago, Chicago, Illinois

John W. Shreve, Assistant Superintendent, Department of Special Services, Cincinnati Public Schools, Cincinnati Ohio

William T. Smith, Jr., Assistant Superintendent, Turner Branch School Building, St. Louis, Missouri

Frederick Williams, Director, Human Relations Unit, Board of Education of the City of New York, Brooklyn, New York

The discussions were recorded, and originally it was intended to publish a summary of the proceedings; however, after the proceedings of the conference were circulated among its members, the decision was made to circulate these materials separate from the publication of the papers.

The conference was made possible through a grant from the Office of Juvenile Delinquency and Youth Development, Welfare Administration, U. S. Department of Health, Education and Welfare in cooperation with the President's Committee on Juvenile Delinquency and Youth Crime. The papers from the conference do not necessarily represent the policies of the sponsoring agency.

Quite a number of people contributed to the conference in addition to the contributors to papers and the school administrators already named. Morris Janowitz and Robert Vinter served as chairmen of sessions. Judy McEndarfer was especially helpful in making conference arrangements and together with her sister, Sharon McEndarfer, provided valuable clerical assistance in the preparation of this volume. The Office of the President, The University of Michigan, generously provided Inglis House for the conference.

Though I assume major responsibility for the theme of the conference, the selection of participants at the conference and the editorial work on this volume, any success as well as failure in achieving the original goal must be shared collectively as well as distributively.

ALBERT J. REISS, JR.

Ann Arbor, Michigan

CONTENTS

Preface   v

1. SCHOOLS IN A CHANGING SOCIETY
   An Introduction, by *Albert J. Reiss, Jr.*, University
   of Michigan   1

2. ORGANIZATIONAL DISPARITY IN DEFINITIONS
   OF DEVIANCE AND USES OF AUTHORITY:
   POLICE, PROBATION, AND THE SCHOOLS
   by *E. K. Nelson, Jr.*, University of Southern California   21

3. ADMINISTRATION STYLES AND COMMUNITY
   LINKAGES OF PUBLIC SCHOOLS: SOME THEO-
   RETICAL CONSIDERATIONS
   by *Eugene Litwak* and *Henry J. Meyer*, University
   of Michigan   49

4. THE YOUTH CULTURE, THE SCHOOL SYSTEM,
   AND THE SOCIALIZATION COMMUNITY
   by *Ronald Lippitt*, University of Michigan   99

5. READING: LARGE ISSUES, SPECIFIC PROBLEMS,
   AND POSSIBLE SOLUTIONS
   by *S. Alan Cohen*, Mobilization for Youth, New
   York City   121

6. ADMINISTRATIVE IMPLICATIONS OF INTEGRA-
   TION PLANS FOR SCHOOLS: OPEN ENROLL-
   MENT IN NEW YORK CITY
       by *Eleanor Bernert Sheldon, James R. Hudson,* and
       Raymond A. Glazier, The Russell Sage Foundation   153

7. CONTEMPORARY SCHOOL PROBLEMS AND PUB-
   LIC POLICY
       by *G. Franklin Edwards,* Howard University   191

   Index   215

Schools in a Changing Society

SCHOOLS IN A CHANGING SOCIETY

AN INTRODUCTION

Albert J. Reiss, Jr.

Today's administrators of our schools are well aware of the many pressures to change their organization and their environment. They see these pressures originating in changes in the community and in the larger society—in changing laws, changing institutions, and even in changing inputs, changes in youth. Ours is a society in which there is rapid technological change. Ours is a world of widespread political upheaval and social unrest. It also is one where most of the controlling institutional forms of organization become more and more specialized through differentiation, and, as we often say, bureaucratic. But the ubiquity of change in modern society need not obscure the fact that some parts of it change more rapidly than others. Some of the established institutions and organizations are more resistant to change than others.

The main organizational goal of the public schools in American society is to educate the young—to change them from illiterate to literate, from the economically dependent to ones capable of entry into a labor market, and, even more broadly, to socialize them into the various civic roles of modern man. To educate is to transfer a resource that is neither expended in transfer nor exhausted through continued use; it is to change people by the addition of knowledge and interpersonal skills.

It is an anomaly that our mass educational systems are among the more slowly changing organizations in our society despite the fact that the process of education remains potentially one of the more powerful means to change people and their organizations. A recurrent theme behind recent changes in American public school systems is that substantial system change comes largely as a response to external crises and organized efforts rather than as a response to definitions of problems generated within school systems. There are the changes in the mathematics curricula following Sputnik, the racial desegregation of public schools following the May 1954 decision of the United States Supreme Court, and the programs of cultural enrichment following those sponsored by the Ford Foundation, among others.

Administrators commonly hear a number of indictments of the public schools. Schools reflect only some consensual elements in communities and not others. They are a main bulwark of institutionalized inequality in the system, inasmuch as they are more likely to buttress the conservative elements in the American social-class and racial-stratification systems than are many labor unions or corporations. Schools, it is said, are under the sway of the professionals. There are the professional administrators who determine everything from the organization of the physical plant to the curricula and the discipline of the clients. There are the licensed teachers who are responsive to the professional schools of education and the professional associations of educators. And there are the professional counselors who advise the students on a vocation and their personal or academic problems.

These professionals are generally accountable only to a part-time board of citizens elected on a nonpartisan basis from the school community. That the board often may be co-opted by the professionals seems clear. That the clients of the school—the parents and more immediately their children—have only limited access to the school and in-direct influence on its policies and practices also seems clear. Indeed, the main avenue of influence on the professionals open to citizens and parents lies in forming pressure groups. Interestingly enough, pressure groups exerting the greatest impact on the organization of schools and on the profes-sionals who operate them in the long run appear to be those that lie outside the immediate environment of the school. The various organizations that meet under school auspices such as parent-teacher organizations also are generally co-opted by it.

These indictments of the school and its administrators lead to a perspective of the school as an embattled organiza-tion, yet one where the professionals are mainly in control. The papers in this volume prepared for the conference gen-erally take a somewhat different perspective. The main goal of the conference was to emphasize that schools, like all organizational systems, must engage in transactions with their environment. This is more apparent in the changing environment of our times. Yet, as Mr. Gross points out, the main characteristics of the school superintendent's role in-herently are those that relate him to the environment outside the school.[1] The top administrators of any major organiza-tion become experts in "foreign" as well as "domestic" relations. For it is they who primarily are responsible for relating the organization to the external environment.

The common thread among the conference papers is their common concern with the school and its relationship to an environing system, an environment consisting of other organizations and institutional arrangements, and changes in them. Organizational aspects of schools and their environment are selected for treatment, particularly as they relate to concerns of top administrators in a school system. We turn now to the general orientation of the conference to the school as an organizational system engaged in transactions with an environment.

§   Adaptive Responses of Schools to Their Environment

Schools are involved in transactions with an environment of organizational systems. They are involved in transactions with organizations that affect their resource base, that affect the source, location, and goals of their clients, and that compete with their socialization goals. We shall briefly examine some consequences of these organizational relationships for school administrators.

Schools deal with youth, and youth have all sorts of problems. These problems are more than just school problems. They are problems of cultural and economic deprivation, of autonomy and dependence, of conformity and deviation from social norms or expectations. There perhaps was a time when schools served only the educational function. That clearly no longer is the case in our larger school systems; and it is doubtful whether teachers ever fulfilled a strictly pedagogical role. Rather, what has changed over time is that schools were forced to extend themselves into a formal organization of these relationships with youth. Where formerly they could treat youth on an informal basis, they now make formal provisions. In fact, our public schools vary considerably in the degree to which they make formal provision for meeting the nonacademic problems of pupils.

The formal ways that schools have adapted to external and internal pressures to meet the problems of youth are themselves of interest. Generally the school has responded to these pressures by introducing specialists within the school system to deal with these problems. Such specialists include the special-education teachers, the professional counselors, and the attendance officers. School systems generally fail to give formal status to their relationships with other agencies in the community whether those of the police, the court, the industrial corporation, the planning commission, the social agency, or a civil rights group. In sum, schools do not actively involve themselves with other organizations at the organizational level. Involvement, when it occurs, comes through the relationships that their specialists establish with employees in other organizations. At the organizational level, the school remains a relatively autonomous organization.

Even where school systems have made some effort to develop relationships with other organizations or groups, they display a preference for co-opting the representative of an organization within the school. Some schools, for example, now permit a member of the police department to be assigned to the school to work with the specialists in the school, but there are no formal relationships between the police department and the school system. Above all, relationships between families and school people are based largely on official commands that bring parents into schools where the professionals control the relationship.

School officials have been selective not only in the

kind of relationship they develop with other organizations but in the type of problem to which they will attend. The school, as noted, is one of a set of deviance defining and processing organizations. Until quite recently, its principal concern was with problems of student conduct or normative deviation. This arose quite naturally from its concern with the regular attendance of the student in school and the behavior problems that pupils present to school officials and teachers while attending school. Its main concern then was to establish relationships with units that shared its common concern with the normative or moral socialization of youth and the control of deviance. Apart from the family, the school is most likely to be involved with organizations for the control of deviance.

The paper by Professor E. K. Nelson, Jr., in this volume emphasizes that organizations dealing with youth in the community have conflicting sets of goals determining the normative ways they will react to the deviance of youth. Thus the police have as their goal the enforcement of the law, the schools that of education, and the probation officer that of rehabilitation. In dealing with youth, the school often will work more closely with the police than with the social worker, given its emphasis on the control of deviance. At the very least, given their diverse emphases in primary goals for their clients, the stage is set for conflict among them.

The problem for the school administrator, as for administrators in each of the agencies dealing with youth, is that there are few formally structured ways that they may work together. Each organization operates essentially as an autonomous unit. The problem from an organizational perspective is one of balancing a common interest in the client with an interest in maintaining organizational autonomy. The school has tended to respond to this situation, as noted, by maintaining organizational autonomy through co-opting representatives of other organizations or by employing its own professionals. Yet inevitably school officials are forced to recognize the claims of others, claims that might be met better, as Professor Nelson suggests, through some organizational solution such as a federation or organizations dealing with youth.

The school is necessarily drawn into relations with organizations and groups in the larger community. Apart from the political organization of the community, schools are one of the few arenas for contest over values and their implementation, and for the resolution of conflict. Indeed, the school, and, above all, its athletic teams, is one of the few remaining symbols of community in the modern metropolis.

It is altogether evident that the school increasingly has become an arena not only for contest over what values are to be taught, but for the contest of wider communiy issues in housing, employment, prejudice, and discrimination. Actually, at the present time in American society, pedagogical issues have so receded into the background, that professional educationalists, such as S. Allen Cohen, defend the primary goal of the school as to teach students how to read and how to acquire knowledge.

Issues over residential segregation become issues in school desegregation. Issues of school desegregation challenge values about local, i.e., neighborhood, schools. Issues about employment opportunities and the class structure of American society become issues in education of the culturally deprived. Such issues, in turn, get translated into issues of local versus federal control of the educational system. The paper by G. Franklin Edwards emphasizes that in all these cases the school, as an organization, fails to define them actively and to relate the school system to them through experimental or innovative practices. The source of this lag lies in part in the structural relations of the school as an organizational system to others of the larger community. Its progressive differentiation from the larger community has brought with it few organized ways that it may deal with organizations having similar problems. Thus, although it has a stake in the development, location, and policies of public housing in the community, it can exercise little impact on them. Its policies in these areas must be geared primarily to a reactive rather than to proactive strategy.

At the same time, the problem lies, in part, in the internal organization of the school. One way that an organization may relate itself to its environment is through the development of research and planning units with long-range plans. An examination of any U.S. public school system shows that the planning function is conceived in very limited ways and that there are restrictive organizational provisions for these functions.

Research departments in schools are primarily focused around major operating problems of a curriculum and its implementation. Many, in fact, are no more than limited intelligence systems for school administrators and teachers, collecting information on student abilities and performance, on school personnel, and on fiscal operations. Where this intelligence system is linked to the planning function, it also may obtain information on community growth and population movement.

These functions themselves are limited, however, by the objectives of the planning department. If one examines the objectives of planning departments in public school systems, one generally finds that their objectives are of three sorts—planning the location and physical construction of schools, fiscal planning, and planning the curricula of students. Even these are short range.

Put in another way, a school generally fails to engage in long-range social planning, beginning with an assessment of the changes underway in the society—the major social trends—then defining its own major goals for its clients, and moving to the implementation of these goals through organizational solutions. Rather, a school responds to crises created by pressures of interest groups to implement the goals of *those* specific groups, and to its own professional ideology and commitments—ones largely generated in professional schools of education and professional associations. In short, the school tends to react to its own environment rather than to actively shape it. This tendency is so marked in school organizational systems that they are in no way prepared for pressures originating in major social issues, even when these have already entered the arena of social conflict. The examples of school segregation, of dropouts, and of increased demands for education in numbers and quality or years of schooling serve as examples of the ways that social planning takes place in our major school systems.

Until the United States Supreme Court's decision on racial segregation, no public school system had any plans to deal with the problems of racial segregation, though a few had responded previously to local pressures to do so. Even when the decision came, most school systems, whether in the North or the South, waited until there were pressures for "a plan." When these first plans appeared, they were primarily statements of principles rather than being an operational statement of goal implementation. The public school system of New York City, as Eleanor Bernert Sheldon and her collaborators show in their paper on desegre-

gation in New York, may serve as an illustration. The first
New York plan was but a general statement affirming belief
in the desirability of racially desegregated schools. Each
succeeding plan became more and more concrete as the
school board and its chief administrative officers were forced
into some form of implementation. The necessity for continually issuing "new plans" arises less from changes in the
short period of time between plans than it does from the
fact that there never has been any long-range plan with
specific proposals on means for implementation of it.[2]

Furthermore, many of the short-range programs actually proposed or implemented may make little sense in
terms of long-range changes underway in New York City.
For example, the ethnic and racial changes underway in
New York—the basic population changes as a consequence
of larger changes in the society—make programs of ethnic
or racial balance in schools sound not only difficult of
achievement but in some cases impossible in the long run.
The implications seem clear. School problems are an aspect
of problems that include residential segregation, poverty,
and lack of opportunity. Unless school planning takes place
within the context of long-range social planning, schools
will continue to react to specific public pressures and interest groups, many of which may actively involve them
in conflicting objectives.

The so-called school dropout problem may serve as a
second illustration of how the organization is drawn into
transactions with an environment. The very language itself
suggests something about the problem. From one organizational perspective, the school dropout is a "force out," one
rejected by the school as an organizational system. The way
that the school is structured to define and handle academic

achievement itself plays an important part in creating a category of students who leave school before completion of their academic program. Those who leave school become a dropout problem when the environment defines these persons as troublesome because they left school before completing its program. The environment then exerts pressures on the school to keep them in and forces young persons to maintain the role of student in the society because the latter lacks alternatives for dealing with them. The basic issue in a sense is not dropouts, but what kind of educational program is necessary for youth in a changing society, and what kinds of opportunities are available to them when they leave school after achieving a given level of schooling?

Failure to define the problem in this broader perspective has implications for the organizational solutions attempted by the school. One organizational solution adopted by schools is to see the problem as one of motivating the student to perform, failing thereby to see that motivation may be closely linked to opportunities in the environment outside the school. Other schools define it as a problem of providing a technical education—the older solution indeed was a special technical or vocational school—but technical education is closely linked to a system of occupations and to job openings in a labor market. The role of industrial and trade unions in structuring labor markets and job systems cannot be scanted in this respect. Yet, typically the school has no organized relationships with such groups in the community.

Reduction of the dropouts from a school system complicates the adaptive response of the school and its administration to its environment. Their retention can markedly affect both the quality and quantity of education. In some lower-class schools it may serve only to widen further the gap between their graduates and the educated elites of the society.

Public school systems generally centralize authority in those areas where it is essential that there be standardization across individual operating units. Authority is centralized in an administrator, as of personnel, or in a professional specialist, as of a curriculum or testing program. Nevertheless, there is considerable delegation of authority within schools systems, particularly to the operating administrator of schools, the principal. Authority is delegated to principals (or, perhaps more accurately, it resides in them by default) in matters relating the school to the immediate local-community environment. The principal and teachers are primarily responsible for dealing with the problems of their clients—parents and pupils—and other agents of the community that have transactions with these clients or school personnel.

The structure of authority in American public school systems resembles in some respects that of a feudal system, the principal occupying somewhat the position of a feudal lord. The paper by Eugene Litwak and Henry Meyer concerns itself with the relationships that schools in a system develop with families and neighborhood organizations and groups. Three major types of administrative relationships or styles of relating the school to the community—the "locked door," the "open door," and "balanced coordination"—and the mechanisms administrators use in each case are described and analyzed. They develop the thesis that these differences in administrative styles between school and community have important consequences for the careers of pupils.

The feudal character of schools can also be seen by

examining the way that parent-teacher organizations are co-opted by the local school. Parent-teacher organizations serve two major functions for the local school. On the one hand the principal can effectively use them to implement school policies vis-à-vis parents; on the other, they serve as his private pressure group against the superintendent and, if necessary, the school board. They become thereby an instrument for local competition in the system. It is rare that the loose federation of parent-teacher organizations becomes effective beyond the level of the local school, given the investment principals have in maintaining their purely local interests. Their very absence in many lower-class urban environments is mute testimony not only to the professional-client, or community-school, environmental relations in lower-class residential areas but to the barrier to equality among schools in the system. One of the surprising things to school administrators in the school desegregation controversy was the effectiveness such lower-class groups can have when they are organized against the professionals in the schools.

Perhaps the most commonly perceived issue in American education is that of local autonomy versus extralocal control. The issue is defined in terms of the government and administration of the school system. It is fraught with all the polemical elements of political controversy. Some of the papers in this volume try to make clear that at the organizational level the matter is not simply one of political autonomy.

The paper by Edwards calls attention to the fact that local systems often fail to provide the organizational flexibility and scope for change necessitated by the changing conditions in the larger society. Schools and the business they are about extends beyond the local community. The problems schools face are not local; indeed, in most cases they lie beyond it. In fact, not only do the resources necessary to their solution on the average lie beyond the local resource base, or at least their power to command them, but the kind of planning and innovation, too, necessary to an educational system in a rapidly changing society lies beyond the professional capabilities and resources of local areas.

Whatever strengths local school systems have had historically, it is clear that they increasingly are subject to external control, whether at the state or federal level. Such extralocal organizational solutions have generally been effected through fiscal control, or through state boards of education controlling curriculum, professional education, and certification and examinations. There is no seamless web of organization controlling public, much less private, education in American society. Rather a loosely coordinated and controlled set of relatively autonomous public and private, professional and lay, political and civic, organizations and associations exert pressures on local school systems.

§   Innovation and Organizational Adaptation

Public schools in American society are an aspect of local and state government. They are formally organized and independent of other forms of local government. Generally a school board elected on a nonpartisan basis is formally charged with their organization and operation. The school board operates the school system.

The rapid growth in size of public school systems fostered in large part by external pressures to consolidate smaller units or as a result of population growth within a district leads to the formal delegation of the operation of the system to an administrator. In the larger public school system such administrators are formally trained in schools of education as professional school administrators. Formally the board retains the role of the formation of policy, though in practice it generally reacts to administrative proposals for educational policy. Yet whenever there is a conflict between the public and the professionals, it is the board that must decide.

Despite this formal separation of powers, it would be mistaken to assume that the structured system, whether under the aegis of the elected officials or the professional administrators, does not reflect adaptation to external as well as internal demands. Moreover, the demands of both professional administrators and elected officials are mediated by the structured system itself. The organization of the school system imposes structured constraints on the continuing adaptation of the organization to internal and external demands. It is to these that we now turn.

The charge often is made that the schools are unresponsive to innovation and it is relatively easy to document in given examples that that is the case. What is not as apparent is how the structured system imposes constraints on innovation or makes them fail. To innovate generally requires alteration in structure—alterations that are not as readily made. A few examples may suffice to illustrate how such constraints must be taken into account in decisions by administrators or teachers to innovate in the system. The paper by Ronald Lippitt in this volume provides other examples.

Curriculum modification may serve as a case in point. Generally the elementary school is structured around a system of grades, or at least one where movement through the system is based on graded achievement or mastery. For this very reason, every significant change at a level below the top level in the system must be evaluated in terms of its effect on levels above it. The very being of this hierarchical organization serves as an effective barrier to much innovation by individual teachers in a system. For the performance of teachers is rated in part by how well prepared her products are for the next higher level in the system. As any curriculum specialist knows well, what is defined as an integrated curriculum is largely one where the presumption can be made that prior achievement has taken place.

A teacher who innovates, therefore, is largely limited to innovation in areas where the presumption of past achievement is unnecessary. For this reason much innovation in public schools occurs either in interpersonal relationships, extracurricular matters, or in situations where mastery is not subsequently open to evaluation. The paper by Lippitt in this volume focuses on some kinds of innovation that in practice can operate within the structural constraints imposed by the system.

Innovation is influenced not only by the hierarchical structure of the school but also by conditions of pupil transfer in and out of systems. A society of high residential mobility itself generates requirements for a standardized system of education. Any school with high in and out mobility of pupils must be able to operate on the presumption that students at a given level have had roughly equivalent kinds of training. A high rate of mobility usually means that significant changes in educational means must occur among all like units in the system. At the same time it means that any changes within a system that do not also prevail beyond the particular system involve costs to it.

The addition of a foreign-language requirement at the

elementary-education level may serve as an example. If only one elementary school in a system adopts a foreign-language requirement, it immediately means that pupil-transfer rates will necessitate either ungraded language courses or beginning courses for new pupils at each grade level. Where other systems do not adopt a foreign-language requirement it will invariably mean that more beginning courses will be required. Thus the school will be forced to adapt its foreign-language curriculum to system differences in curriculum requirements. Under such conditions, in the long run the system will tend to coerce system-wide adoption, or the innovation will fail to survive.

Innovation in the schools likewise is markedly influenced by the way in which the role of the teacher is structured both by the profession and by the organization of the school. Generally in American schools, a teacher is prepared for a specialized role. At the elementary level this means that she is prepared to teach at certain grade levels and not others. Furthermore, her job will tend to coerce specialization even further. She is prepared, for example, to be a second-grade teacher. To become a third-grade teacher means that she must expend additional effort to do so. She must prepare new outlines and projects and master new materials. The system will generally work then toward stabilizing a teacher at a given grade level.

Suppose, therefore, as was the case in a project in Quincy, Illinois, that it was desired to have the teacher relate to the same pupils and their families over time. She was asked to work with the families in their homes as well as with the pupils in school. Ignoring for the moment the fact that such an innovation might be resisted because of difficulties in getting professionals to structure a role in changing environments (the school after all has the advantage that the professionals can largely manipulate the environment) the fact remained that an innovation that would leave the pupils with the same teacher for his entire period of elementary education would require the teacher to be responsible for six or seven levels of education rather than for one. Strangely enough such a teacher would over a period of time be like the teacher in a one-room rural school. At this point it perhaps is unnecessary to state that even with the support of administrators, this innovation failed because the teachers resisted the pressures to change their grade level each year. They refused to be "promoted" along with the students, citing professional, i.e., specialized competence, as a basis.

Educators, particularly of the psychological persuasion, have regarded the learning situation as one in which the teachers teach pupils how to learn and what he learns. Over time it has become apparent that there is a classroom environment [3] and indeed a school environment that includes, among other elements, a peer-organized system. Much of the literature on the peer system in schools focuses on how the peer system interferes with the educational goals of the teacher, particularly through the organization of deviant subcultures. The paper by Professor Lippitt shows ways that the peer system may be integrated with the learning environment.

§   Epilogue

The papers that follow in this volume concern themselves primarily with the school as an organizational system. They raise a number of problems that confront schools as organizations—regarding them as responding rather than innovating agents, forces of conservation more than of change, isolated and autonomous rather than involved institutions in the community and society. They show a common concern with ways that the organizational system may adapt to the environment. They raise questions and problems in organizational adaptation to a rapidly changing society.

Notes

1. Neal Gross, W. S. Mason, and A. W. McEachern, *Explorations in Role Analysis* (New York: John Wiley & Sons, 1958); also, *Who Runs Our Schools?* (New York: John Wiley & Sons, Inc., 1958).

2. To be sure, the failure of schools to plan for desegregation results not only from the lack of organizational provision for it but in many cases from their very relationship to controversial issues, a relationship that tends to affirm the *status quo*.

3. Talcott Parsons, "The School Class as a Social System: Some of Its Functions in American Society," *Harvard Educational Review*, XXIX (Fall, 1959), 297-318.

2

ORGANIZATIONAL DISPARITY
IN DEFINITIONS OF DEVIANCE
AND USES OF AUTHORITY

POLICE, PROBATION, AND THE SCHOOLS

E. K. Nelson, Jr.

§   Introduction

Adolescent social deviance, an immensely diverse set
of behaviors, elicits widely differing reactions from the various subsystems of the community responsible for treatment
or control of the problem. Little attention has been given
to these institutional differences in defining and coping with
adolescent deviance—regarding either the effect of inconsistent applications of authority on the youth involved or
the relationships among the subsystems and between them
and the larger community.

The Youth Studies Center of the University of Southern California has conducted studies of the handling of
socially deviant youth by a number of community agencies.[1]
This paper draws upon collected data concerning the police,

probation, and the schools. A profile of attributes is posited
for each of these types of organization, with reference to
their normative ways of defining and acting toward adolescent deviance. Consideration then is given to the effects of
discongruity between the institutions on their relationships
with youth, with each other and with the more generalized
social system of the community. Some examples of interaction between representatives of police, probation, and school
organizations are taken from a Youth Studies Center experiment in which a diversified set of community opinion leaders
was asked to plan a comprehensive program for delinquency
prevention on the basis of information supplied by the
Center concerning the nature of youth problems and needs.[2]
Still another source of "case study" material is an incident
of sharp disagreement between a police and a probation
organization concerning the operation of programs for delinquent groups.[3]

William Dienstein investigated conflict in beliefs among
police, probation, and school personnel, about the causes
of delinquency, and concluded that:

> . . . while each agency is dealing with delinquency and each
> may handle the same violator, their approaches to the same
> problem tend to take on polar aspects—control and punish-
> ment on the one hand, and treatment on the other—and
> they find no route to mutual understanding, communication
> and cooperation. Working thus at cross purposes, they cannot
> hope to succeed.[4]

Dienstein's conclusion that disharmony in goals and modes
of operation does in fact exist, and that it is dysfunctional
to the organizations involved seems to be characteristic of
the views of various observers who effect a neutral position
or purport to speak for some transcendent interest such as

"the whole community" or "the welfare of youth." But to decry the organizational decision makers for failing to co-operate with each other does not increase understanding of either the causes or the consequences of the differences which exist.

Two major and polemical systems of belief serve as possible referents for community institutions which need to define and deal with adolescent deviance. One is, in essence, a *free will* position, which holds the individual responsible for "wrong" conduct and relies on punishment both to deter and reform. The other is a form of *determinism*, which stresses social and psychic causes of social deviance and argues for programs of treatment and prevention. Community opinion, as expressed in the mass media, is highly ambivalent and fluctuating in the face of these opposed philosophies.

Organizations which contact deviant youth must oper-ate mainly according to one system or the other (as do the police and probation), or become settings (as do the schools) for conflict between competing systems of beliefs. How community subsystems committed to varying patterns of free will, determinism, and conflict can cooperate to de-velop a better definition of adolescent deviance and more consistent policies of dealing with deviants is a question of great social importance. One approach to this question is to examine the kinds of reciprocity and conflict which exist among the institutions involved.

No doubt the primary purpose of each organization determines to a great extent its ways of reacting to deviance in the "client" group. Thus, law enforcement, education, and rehabilitation each create strong and distinctive organiza-tional imperatives. Function and purpose, for example, make it "logical" for the police officer to explain deviance in terms

of free will, and for probation officers to use deterministic
explanations. But these distinctions often are blurred since
rehabilitation sometimes requires law enforcement, law enforcement sometimes involves assistance with personal and
social problems, and education frequently has elements
of both law enforcement and assistance. Indeed, there is
interesting evidence that authority figures who interact
with youth in all the types of organizations under discussion
find appropriate ways to carry out non-normative functions;
e.g., the police counsel and probation officers discipline
some of the youth they contact.[5]

Alvin Gouldner, agreeing with Talcott Parsons that
"the most general and fundamental property of a system is
the interdependence of parts or variables," nevertheless
argues that there are varying degrees of interdependence
and that the problem of asymmetrical patterns of reciprocity
between parts of a social system (as police, probation, and
school organizations are parts of a community) has been
neglected.[6] Gouldner suggests questions pertinent to understanding organizational disparity in defining deviance and
using authority. For example: When reciprocity breaks
down between the institutional systems involved, what
compensatory mechanisms (perhaps through independent
social structures) can perform the functions of communication, arbitration, and adjudication? Are there "hidden"
reciprocities between subsystems whose relationships are
otherwise characterized by tension and competition? Are
there functional as well as dysfunctional effects in the
capacity of the larger social system to insulate the parts
from each other, protecting as well as linking them within
the network? Perhaps most significantly in terms of the
ambiguous definitions of crime and punishment, Gouldner
leads us to ask whether a confederation of interests among

police, probation, school, and other institutions may not be more satisfactory than maximizing cooperation and, if so, what strategies may organization decision makers follow to gain limited cooperative objectives without jeopardizing the integrity of the institutional systems they represent. We will consider these questions after making certain postulations about the normative system of the police, probation, and schools in defining and handling adolescent deviance.

§   Profiles of Organization Norms

The Police

The police officer can say with justice that "the buck stops here" when he deals with social deviance.[7] His actions, often taken in a context of ugliness and danger, must be specific and direct, and yet he often must account for what he did to varied audiences who use vastly differing criteria in judging him.

John M. Pfiffner has investigated the role of the police in dealing with juveniles during the past two years. His work indicates that law enforcement as a subsystem of the community holds a modal position with regard to defining and acting toward adolescent deviance, a position which is quite close to the free will pole of the "accountability" versus "determinism" continuum. Granted that the police position occupies a range rather than a point on the continuum (for example, specialists in juvenile work seem less punitive than other police personnel, and officers on the beat make concessions to the principle of helping and treating offenders that some top police administrators are not prepared to make), still the police belief system is mainly a moralistic judgment that deviant conduct is willful and should be met

with stern penalties, adamantly applied. Indeed, there is
evidence of an increasingly strong attitude among the police
that most of society is woefully "soft" in dealing with offenders, and that the professionals committed to helping
and treating deviants are instigators of this social laxity.
Pfiffner says:

> Do the police tend to think didactically? Do they see issues
> in terms of black and white and take positions which they
> regard as morally correct, becoming intolerant of counter
> viewpoints, sometimes with emotional involvement? One
> evidence of this emerges from what would seem to be a
> general police attitude toward motivation of criminal be-
> havior and the causes of crime. In general, environmental
> causes are either rejected or minimized and the classical
> viewpoint of free will and inherent cussedness accepted.
> There would seem to be a predilection toward moralizing;
> the home, the church and other such institutions have failed
> to maintain moral guidance and have abdicated to the police
> their proper duty to maintain discipline. In this sense the
> police regard themselves as the final resort in handling the
> cases symptomatic of the failures of society. They look back
> nostalgically to a perhaps legendary age when tne folk
> culture and the family were strong factors in maintaining
> social order. Thus the police may regard themselves as the
> custodians of a public conscience to which society gives only
> lip service. The term "last puritans" has been applied to the
> police. . . .[8]

In the spring of 1963, the chief of police of the City
of Los Angeles and the sheriff of Los Angeles County made
headlines by protesting to the Board of Supervisors about
the activities of the Group Guidance Unit of the County
Probation Department, a group of deputies working directly
with delinquent gangs rather than using more traditional

casework techniques with individual offenders. The Youth
Studies Center was in a good position to document the
effects of this action, since it had a research team in the field
evaluating the work of the Group Guidance Unit. The incident highlights the police position and provides a revealing
study of the consequences of an effort to assert that position
aggressively in the community.

The chief and the sheriff said, in effect, that group
guidance operations increased rather than reduced delinquency and that delinquent gangs should be dissipated
rather than be given greater solidarity through adult intervention and solicitude. Probation, at first shaken by the
attack, sought to mount a counterattack. The Board of
Supervisors meantime suspended the group-guidance
program.

The events that followed were revealing in regard to
the issues under discussion here, partly because the ensuing
dialogue between the two organizations highlighted their
predilections, and partly because the compromise that followed (quite literally defined as a truce) illustrated the
untenability of polar positions on the *free-will-determinism*
continuum once diverse interest groups entered the arena
and impinged upon superordinate political echelons.

Following an initial phase in which police and probation argued publicly with each other, both became concerned about indiscriminate attack and support from outside
"fanatics" and established a small truce team composed
of middle-management representatives of the two organizations. Top administrative and political decision makers were
able thus to accept certain negotiated conditions for continued operation of the group-guidance program while
publicly adopting a "wait and see what the research produces" attitude toward the more fundamental and, for now,

irreconcilable questions involved. In Gouldner's terms, one subsystem, the police, provisionally adopted a foreign policy of seeking to reorganize the larger social system to satisfy its distinctive needs more fully. Following the intervention of various outside structures and interests—some highly partisan, others seeking to play the role of arbiter—both factions were more than content to exploit hidden reciprocities, if only temporarily and ostensibly in the interest of seeing that "research gets a chance to come up with some answers."

Probation

The Youth Studies Center began its investigations of probation in 1960 through tape-recorded interviews with adolescent probationers and their probation officers "about each other, about the activities in which officers engage, and about ways in which probation is and should be carried out." [9] Subsequently judges and probation administrators were interviewed on similar subjects. Currently the Center is carrying out research in nine Southern California counties on the relative effectiveness of different dispositions (of youth arrested and referred to probation departments) and supervision practices, against the criterion of re-referral to probation. [10]

The Center's study of probation revealed, among other things, a wide range of values and premises for action among probation officers and administrators. This discovery has led to a rudimentary classification of officers and some hypotheses about matching officers and probationers to achieve more effective treatment. [11] Certainly the dominant belief system of probation organizations about the cause and handling of social deviance is far from monolithic, and probably possesses less consensus than does that of police organizations.[12] T. C. Esselstyn, arguing that there "is a net-work of social relations (among corrections personnel) sufficiently lasting and detailed to be called a social sys-tem," [13] makes the interesting observation that the primary relations of probation personnel are with fellow workers, and their relations with probationers are derivative and less precisely defined.

Nevertheless, all evidence indicates that the modal position of probation in defining and handling adolescent deviance is well toward the determinism pole of the free-will-determinism continuum. Moreover, the deterministic explanation most heavily favored in the probation belief system is that individual aberrations are the primary cause of criminal deviance and that psychotherapy forms the basis of treatment. Esselstyn says of probation officers, "their knowledge of cause is already determined by the system, and the system is so heavily committed to individualistic explanations that few other approaches [e.g., sociocultural interpretations of the cause of crime] can get a hearing." [14]

The commitment of probation to understanding and treating, rather than to detecting and punishing, social de-viance is reflected in the following statement from a pro-bation administrator asked to describe the *best* probation officer he has ever known.

In terms of know-how . . . I've heard him again and again in meetings bring forth the real basic dynamics in cases that he was handling; and not only this but with other officers . . . he had this uncanny ability without even know-ing the kid, just by way of explanation by someone else . . . of picking out the real basic factors. . . . We used to call him Doc.[15]

Addressing judges at an institute on: "What Is Good

Juvenile Court Probation?", Eugene H. Burns drew upon a literary source to emphasize a similar view of the mission of probation:

> I would like to close with a quotation from Harper Lee's novel, *To Kill A Mockingbird*. A young girl, Scout, is talking with her father the lawyer. . . .
> "First of all," he said, "if you can learn a simple trick, Scout, you'll get along a lot better with all kinds of folks. You never really understand a person until you consider things from his point of view. . . ."
> "Sir?"
> ". . . until you climb into his skin and walk around in it." [16]

Within the large community, probation has experienced great difficulty in communicating and gaining acceptance for its view of social deviance. "Understanding and treating" seem to be less satisfying to the public than do "apprehending and punishing." In describing earlier an incident of conflict between police and probation organizations we noted that the police initially asserted their position on deviance aggressively through the public media. Probation was much less assertive in seeking to preserve its autonomy, despite demands from lower organizational echelons and certain citizen groups that a vigorous and compelling case be made for the "treatment approach." In Gouldner's terms, the essential strategy of probation (though not necessarily devised through a process of rational analysis and decision) was *withdrawal* from public conflict and neutralization of extreme attacks through such tactics as appeal to higher authority, behind-the-scenes persuasion, and reliance on the passage of time to "cool" the situation. [17]

The Schools

Cicourel and Kitsuse point out that:

The school system may be conceived as an organization which produces, in the course of its activities, a variety of adolescent careers including the delinquent. Within the organizational setting of the school, the day-to-day activities of adolescents and personnel define, classify, and process a wide range of "routine" and "problem" behavior. Because the school occupies a strategic position as a coordinating agency between the activities of the family, the police, and the peer group vis-à-vis adolescents, it also provides a "clearing house" which receives and releases information from and to other agencies concerning adolescents." [18]

During the past four years, the Youth Studies Center has carried on research and experimentation on the school's role in adolescent socialization and re-socialization. A sample of 300 male adolescents, consisting of "aggressive" (deviants from the school rule-system), "passive underachieving," and "well-adjusted" subgroups, has been followed through their high school careers with the purpose of identifying differential effects of the school organization in facilitating or impeding preparation for effective performance of adult roles and responsibilities.[19] This study focused upon factors which influenced academic and social adjustment during adolescence.

In addition, the Center has participated in an action-research program in which 30 boys classified as "aggressive" and "passive underachievers" were placed in special classes where they received a modified curriculum, intensive counseling, and a part-time, paid job.[20] This program included:
(1) a single teacher for all subjects;
(2) low teacher-pupil ratio [Conditions (1) and (2) pro-

vide a close personal relationship between teacher and
student, and permit the use of reward and punishment
on an individual basis];

(3) special curricula related to the interests of the students
and providing some preparation for their occupational
roles;

(4) curriculum and work assignments adjusted to the level
of skill of each student so that he could perform
successfully;

(5) remedial instruction in basic academic skills;

(6) a special counselor to act as confidante and "safety
valve";

(7) group dynamics techniques (mainly group discussion) to develop a climate conducive to learning;

(8) work experience with pay.

The Center's research findings most pertinent to the
present discussion concern the "aggressive" boys, who were
studied in both the basic and the action-research phases.
There is strong and consistent evidence that overt defiance
of rules and norms within the school social system elicits
predominantly negative sanctions from teachers, deans, and
other authorities. Student aggression threatens the basic
mission of the school to impart knowledge and values. The
school's reaction to disruptive actions may reinforce negative behavior patterns, thereby helping to fulfill the prophecy
of "badness" for certain youth. Visibly deviant boys were
rejected from the social system by their peers (although
not by other aggressives with whom they shared the image
of nonconformist), as well as from the structures, services,
and rewards controlled by adults. Interviews with students
indicated that no school official, even the counselor, was
perceived consistently as a source of assistance with serious
personal problems.[21]

The belief system of the school in regard to defining and handling social deviance seems less well defined than that of either the police or probation. Attitudes vary considerably among teachers, counselors, deans (the major formal disciplinarians), and other personnel in the organizational system. Some teachers are more helpful to deviant youth than are others; some are more sensitive than others to behavior which threatens their authority and control. However, in the face of overt aggression, the system assumes a more well-defined position by denying its resources to the transgressor and conserving them for the "healthy" or conforming student. The absence of resources to implement a nonpunitive policy may be an important factor in this process. As Dienstein's data suggest, the modal position of the school on the free-will-determinism continuum is closer to that of the police than to that of probation.[22]

Thus, the school is more ambiguous in defining the nature and cause of deviance (deterministic as well as punitive interpretations appear frequently) than in acting toward deviance. Lefever has suggested that a contributing factor in this phenomenon is that social deviance is disproportionately manifested within the school by lower-class youth, while teachers and other school authorities largely endorse middle-class values and have little tolerance for or understanding of the behaviors of socially disadvantaged adolescents.[23]

Thomas Gladwin has succinctly characterized the present psychologically based approach to deviant youth as one which makes conformity tolerable,[24] a strategy scarcely designed to effect changes in the cultural and social pattern that produces and reinforces social deviance in some youth. Some recent programs in or ancillary to the school have made the peer group [25] or the learning situation [26] the target

of experimental efforts to induce positive rather than deviant behavior, instead of supposing that individual therapy
(which, aside from questions of its appropriateness, seldom
is available) is the only real answer. Unfortunately, in my
opinion, there has been a paucity of experimentation directed at both the individual *and* his social situation, with
effective linkage and articulation between the two types
of assistance.

Previously in this paper, it was suggested that at times
police organizations seek to maintain or increase their autonomy by imposing their definition of deviance on the
social system, while probation organizations practice a
strategy of limited withdrawal. Now, in an even more specu-
lative vein, Gouldner's third postulated strategy, by which
a subsystem may act to preserve or enhance its autonomy,
will be applied to the schools. This is the strategy of *spreading risks* through partial commitment to a number of belief
systems and community structures.

The school is in a good position to spread risks by "buy-
ing into" a number of competing systems. Its mission of
educating does not demand the same polarity in defining
deviance as that faced by the police in *controlling* or probation in *treating*. In fact, as an institution which must offer
direct service to virtually the entire community, the school
has little choice but to present varied definitions of purpose
and philosophy in order to satisfy (or at least in order not
to alienate) heterogeneous reference groups which have
conflicting expectations of the school. Indeed, one frequently
expressed frustration of school administrators is that of
trying to be all things to all people. This seems to apply
to the general position of the school in regard to adolescent
deviance. Speaking in public situations, school administrators tend to subscribe to better service for *all* youth. But

when the deviant threatens the internal operations of the system, the school's reaction belies such statements.

It should be noted, however, that providing new forms of handling deviance within the school may well modify the operations of the entire subsystem with respect to such problems. This seems especially to be the case when there are clear rewards of professional prestige and public recognition for the school decision maker who not only supports experimental programs for socially deviant youth but also acts to ramify the precepts and learnings of such programs outside of the experimental unit.

Thus, in Youth Studies Center experimentation, three years of operating demonstration programs for aggressive and underachieving youth brought increasing support from school administrators. The importance of such support for the success of the experiment (to say nothing of spreading its effects through the system) is reflected in the fact that initially teachers employed for the demonstration work reported a sense of isolation from their professional peers and a concern about the effects of working with deviants on their standing with administrators and ultimately on their careers.

Efforts to modify the school environment have been directed mainly at teachers, counselors, and others who work directly with the students. We have yet to devise effective approaches to modifying the organizational system of the school. As S. M. Miller says, "Changes at the administrative level make possible and encourage possibilities at the teacher level (and in the office and janitorial roles which are frequently overlooked in their impact upon students) . . . the crucial importance of organizational form and style has been largely ignored." [27]

§   Consequences and Implications of Organizational
Disparity

Reactions of Youth to Discongruity between Subsystems

Laurence Wylie has stated that youth in the United
States come to feel that the rules which govern social behavior are phony and hypocritical. Referring to *Mad* maga-
zine's satires on the American cult of optimism (and contrasting the American authority system with that of France,
where rules and norms allegedly are more clearly defined),
Wylie holds that the plight of the adolescent "lies not in
living up to expectations but in discovering what they
really are." [28] In this context, it seems useful to consider the
reactions of youth to differing institutional definitions of
the cause and handling of deviance.

Recently the Youth Studies Center has experimented in
Santa Monica, California, with a community self-study
strategy through which youth defined by their peers as
leaders were brought together with lay and professional
influentials from the adult power structure to plan a comprehensive program of delinquency prevention. [29] Each of
the three subgroups (youth leaders, lay leaders, and professional leaders) participated separately in twelve hours
of instruction on the general social and economic structure
of their community, on various indicators of youth problems
and needs, and on current patterns of using existing services
and resources for youth. Subsequently, the three types of
leaders were brought together in a three-day retreat to plan
an action program based upon the prior discussions. In
the past year, varied efforts have been used to implement
the recommendations developed through this process; four

content areas have predominated: (1) the development of "reaching out" services to neighborhoods which had many problems and relatively few services; (2) the establishment of special youth-employment programs; (3) the development of a broader base of community understanding and support for needed services; (4) the development of an on-going and indigenous structure to replace the work of the Center by providing for future study, planning and coordinating activities. Substantial accomplishments have been made in all but the last area, in which there continues to be controversy concerning the location and financing of the proposed coordinating mechanism.

This experiment provided an unusual opportunity to observe youth interacting with adult authority figures who represented subsystems with diverse orientations to adolescent deviance. In the main, the boys and girls involved seemed quite sophisticated in understanding the different frames of reference imposed by the distinctive needs of the institutions involved. More significantly, however, the youthful participants frequently served as catalysts and mediators in facilitating communication between adults. They were able to speak with authority and insight from a "recipient's view" of adult interventions, often correcting misconceptions held by their elders. That they had been given the same factual information as the adult participants while having the presence of neutral leadership from the university seemed to be a major factor in freeing the adolescents to take a more active and constructive role than usual in their contacts with adults. The general strategy of using those afflicted with social problems in programs aimed at the diagnosis and solution of those problems seems to have high potential, and is being attempted in an increasing number of experimental approaches to complex human predicaments, including alcoholism, narcotics addiction, and gang-based delinquency.[30]

Another and quite different community program in which adolescents have been major participants is an experiment which has been conducted in Provo, Utah, over the past three years under the direction of LaMar Empey.[31] Making the delinquent-peer group the major target of intervention efforts, and conceiving of interactions among group members as the primary process leading to behavioral change, the Provo researchers collected a rich store of data during group discussions, some bearing upon the members' reactions to the community authority systems with which they were in contact. All the boys participating in this program had been defined by court action as seriously delinquent prior to acceptance, in contrast to the Santa Monica adolescents, who represented a wide range from conforming to nonconforming behavior.

Empey has described the reactions of group members to institutional authority as generally vague and ill-defined, but with variance in modal attitudes toward the police, probation, and the schools. Despite frequent complaints about police actions toward them, the boys were said to understand the belief system of the police more clearly than that of either probation or the schools. Moreover, Empey suggests that normative definitions of the causes and consequences of deviance generated through group discussions among the boys themselves seemed more consonant with the police position than with the deterministic norm of probation. The boys seemed well aware of the need felt by school authorities to protect their system against disruptive behavior, indicating that they could stay out of trouble in that setting by maintaining low visibility. There were strong perceptions among the boys that the authority system of probation (and to a lesser extent that of the schools) invited manipulation, that authority figures who work from deterministic premises can be hoodwinked by "telling them what they want to hear." It should be borne in mind, in interpreting these comments, that the Provo experiment is heavily structured to maximize intervention by the adolescent peer group in the lives of its members, thereby minimizing more conventional interventions by such adult workers as probation officers and school counselors.

In general, youth seem cognizant of differing institutional norms regarding deviance, and make personal adjustments to them with widely varying degrees of skill and acumen. Youth not defined as social deviants (and who do not define themselves as deviants) may understand the plight of their deviant peers more realistically than do adults, perhaps because the youth are sensitive to the strains imposed by inconsistent and shifting expectations. Delinquent youth or those formally defined as deviant tend to develop negative patterns of interaction with authority figures in all systems, but the nature of these interactions varies greatly. The commitment of institutions to free-will or deterministic beliefs regarding deviance seems to be a significant factor in understanding such variance. The Santa Monica and the Provo experiments illustrate efforts to involve both deviant and non-deviant youth in programs aimed at reducing adolescent problems, a strategy which, while little used, has apparent promise.

Relationships among Subsystems and between Subsystems and the Community

In the community, the generalized norm regarding the institutions which serve and control youth is that they

should achieve greater integration in their activities. The
public and the top political and administrative officials are
disturbed when an overt clash (e.g., between police and
probation) makes contradictory values acutely visible. Moreover, outside of the community, those concerned with en-
hancing programs for youth also press for greater "cooperation" and "coordination" between the subsystems. In fact,
private foundations and the federal government, by issuing
grants for planning and demonstration projects, have encouraged metropolitan communities to develop coordinated
structures to deal with youth problems.[32]

The subsystems, on the other hand, are predominantly
concerned with protecting their boundaries and maintaining or strengthening their autonomy. Subsystem officials
endorse the general social norm that cooperation is desirable, but remain oriented to the distinctive needs, functions,
and problems of their specific institutions. When top leadership of a subsystem commits itself to goals of cooperation
and integration, lower bureaucratic levels may negate or
dilute the implementation of such unfamiliar policies, either
by taking actions inconsistent with them or by taking no
action at all. Such insularity is supported by the fact that
career advancement and reward lie within rather than between subsystems, and that networks of communication
and reciprocity also are largely internal, especially at the
lower levels where direct service to youth is effected.

Sometimes negative reciprocal stereotypes develop between those concerned primarily with maintaining subsystem autonomy and those concerned with increasing the
integration of the subsystems (e.g., superordinate official-
dom, representatives of senior governments, and foundation
officials). One might speculate that each regards the other
as perverse because neither understands the imperatives of

the other. In particular, greater understanding is needed of the constraints which inhibit efforts to integrate programs dealing with socially deviant youth. Among the most potent of these constraints are: (1) variance in explanations of deviance (as indicated by the perseverance of the free-will-determinism dichotomy) and (2) the highly differentiated missions assigned to the police, probation, schools, and other youth-serving agencies.

While recognizing the negative consequences of organizational disparity on the stability of the community social system, and the dysfunctional effects of such disparity on youth, there is a need for realism in defining the kinds of integration which are viable, given the fact that the organizations which deal with youth are distributed through several levels of government and draw their financial and ideological support from many sectors of society.[33] The system or coalition of the organizations which deal with youth should be conceived of as a federation of autonomous parts rather than as a unified whole. In addition to promoting mutual exchanges betwen subsystems, the community social system must at times protect the parts from each other (and, one might add from outside interests over-zealous to have them act in concert), Gouldner has suggested that "The system model thus indicated for the analysis of social behavior is not one in which the system is viewed as a 'plunger' playing an all-or-none game, but as a mini-max player seeking to strike a federalizing balance between totalitarian and anarchist limits." [34]

The foregoing view does not question the need for innovations in structure and process to attain more effective collaboration between youth-serving agencies. Nor does it suggest that superordinate and external interests should refrain from sanctioning the norm of coordinated activity.

Instead, it emphasizes the need for realism and "strategic" sophistication in moving to achieve integration, for the development of models of social change which allow vested interests and disparate values their essential place in the system, while setting in motion new patterns of communication and collaboration.

The concept that organizational cooperation in dealing with adolescent deviance must recognize the autonomy drives of the subsystems places a high premium on a type of leadership style and skill which meets specific institutional needs while exploiting opportunities for collaboration. Thus, the head of a police, probation, school, or any other youth-serving organization in the modern metropolis needs to provide at once for "system maintenance" functions and for innovations in working arrangements with other agencies, a mandate which presents many practical dilemmas. When inter-organization communication breaks down, superordinate administrative and political leadership must assume greater responsibility for linking the parts, preventing them from damaging each other irreparably, and asserting the general community interest in efficient reciprocal arrangements. Top leadership has not always been sufficiently "literate" in understanding conflicting institutional imperatives to meet this challenge effectively. Pfiffner suggests that the broadly trained administrator (e.g., professional city managers) may have better strategic and catalytic skills for this purpose than do less politically astute and more functionally oriented administrators.[35]

The very tension and disagreement about ultimate purposes among the subsystems dealing with adolescent deviance today may, paradoxically, be a force in creating new structural and functional devices to connect the parts, to mediate between them, and to isolate those parts of the program which can be carried on through genuinely co-operative arrangements. The discovery of new forms of reciprocity in response to discomforting tensions is one method of effecting social change, and the urgent needs of youth in our time can be expected to maintain pressure on decision makers at all levels.[36]

In many programs designed to effect greater coordination between subsystems the element which seems to have been missing thus far is that of meaningful exploration of current mandates, functions, obligations, and expectations with representatives of all parts involved. Working from a base of facts and agreed-upon perceptions about such matters, and given time to understand their implications across functional lines, subsystem representatives can move in authentic rather than in idealistic ways to identify common ground and, eventually, to enlarge the areas in which they can articulate and multiply their efforts.[37]

Notes

1. E. K. Nelson, Jr., "Program Orientations of a Youth Studies Center," *Sociology and Social Research*, XLVI, No. 4 (July, 1962); Jane Criner, "Use of Authority in the Treatment of Deviant Youth" (Los Angeles: Youth Studies Center, University of Southern California, 1961), Working Paper No. 8.

2. E. K. Nelson, Jr., "The Feedback of Research Information as a Stimulus for the Development of a Delinquency Prevention Program," *Toward a Professional Identity in School Psychology*, Proceedings, Fourteenth Annual Conference, California Association of School Psychologists and Psychometrists, 1963; Herbert R. Sigurdson and Donald G. Dodge, "Social Change as a Function of Community Education," Research Proposal submitted to the National Institute of Mental Health by the Youth Studies Center, University of Southern California (describes a three-year community self-study project to be

undertaken in an ethnically mixed Los Angeles neighborhood beginning in March, 1964).

3. "The Juvenile Gang Debate," Editorial, *Los Angeles Times*, April 8, 1963.

4. William Dienstein, "Conflict of Beliefs about Causes of Delinquency," *Crime and Delinquency*, VI, No. 3 (July, 1960), 293.

5. John M. Pfiffner, "Parameters of the Role of the Police in Dealing with Juveniles" (Los Angeles: Youth Studies Center, University of Southern California, August, 1963), p. 6; A. W. McEachern, *et al.*, "Views of Authority: Probationers and Probation Officers" (Los Angeles: Youth Studies Center, University of Southern California, 1961), Research Paper No. 1, p. 103.

6. Alvin W. Gouldner, "Reciprocity and Autonomy," in Llewellyn Gross (ed.), *Symposium on Sociological Theory* (New York: Harper & Row, Publishers, 1959), 241-66.

7. John P. Kenney, *et al.*, "California Police Training Programs Relating to Juvenile Offenders" (Los Angeles: Youth Studies Center, University of Southern California, 1961), Research Paper No. 3, p. 4.

8. John M. Pfiffner, "The Functions of the Police in a Democratic Society" (Los Angeles: Youth Studies Center, University of Southern California, 1963), pp. 12-13.

9. A. W. McEachern, *et al.*, "Views of Authority: Probationers and Probation Officers," *op. cit.*, p. 213.

10. A. W. McEachern, and William R. Larson, "Probation: Position and the Process" (Research proposal submitted to the National Institute of Mental Health by the Youth Studies Center, University of California). It describes a study of probation in nine Southern California counties begun in the fall of 1963.

11. Ted Palmer, "Types of Probation Officers and Types of Youth on Probation: Their Views and Interactions" (Los Angeles: Youth Studies Center, University of Southern California, 1963), Project Report.

12. Lloyd E. Ohlin, Herman Piven, and Donnel M. Pappenfort, "Major Dilemmas of the Social Worker in Probation and Parole," *National Probation and Parole Association Journal*, II, No. 3 (July, 1956), 213; E. K. Nelson, Jr., "The Gulf Between Theory and Practice in Corrections," *Federal Probation*, XVIII, No. 3 (Sept., 1954), 50.

13. T. C. Esselstyn, "The Social System of Correctional Workers" (unpublished paper presented to meetings of Pacific Sociological Asso-

ciation in Tucson, Arizona, April 15, 1961), p. 1. The author is a Professor of Sociology at San Jose State College, San Jose, Calif.

14. *Ibid*, p. 9.

15. From a transcript of a tape-recorded interview conducted by Professor Norris E. Class with an administrator in the Los Angeles County Probation Department (in the confidential files of the Youth Studies Center, University of Southern California).

16. Eugene H. Burns, "What Is Good Juvenile Court Probation?" *Proceedings: Juvenile Probation Town Meeting for Judges*, Oct. 4-6, 1963 (sponsored by Michigan Probate and Juvenile Judges Association and Children's Charter of the Juvenile Courts of Michigan, Inc., 703 So. Westnedge Ave., Kalamazoo, Mich.), p. 16.

17. Alvin Gouldner, "Reciprocity and Autonomy," *op. cit.*, p. 259.

18. Aaron V. Cicourel and John I. Kitsuse, "The Social Organization of the High School and Deviant Adolescent Careers" (mimeographed paper, approximately 1960).

19. Fred J. Shanley *et al.*, "Comparative Study of Factors Influencing the School Adjustment of Adolescents: A Preliminary Report" (Los Angeles: Youth Studies Center, University of Southern California, 1961), Research Paper No. 2; D. Welty Lefever *et al.*, "Preliminary Analysis of School Records and Behavioral Data for Matched Groups of Aggressive, Well-adjusted, and Underachieving Boys" (Los Angeles: Youth Studies Center, University of Southern California, 1961), Research Paper No. 8.

20. Langdon E. Longstreth, Fred J. Shanley, and Roger E. Rice, "Experimental Evaluation of a High School Program for Potential Dropouts" (presented for publication in December, 1963).

21. William R. Larson, and Roger E. Rice, "The Differential Perception of the School Counselor by Deviant and Non-Deviant Students" (paper presented at the 1963 Annual Meeting of the American Psychological Association, Philadelphia, Pa.). The senior author is a project head at the Youth Studies Center, University of Southern California.

22. William Dienstein, "Conflict of Beliefs about Causes of Delinquency," *op. cit.*

23. D. Welty Lefever, "Research Findings and Needs Relating to the School's Responsibility for Deviant Behavior" (Los Angeles: Youth Studies Center, University of Southern California, 1961), Working Paper No. 1, p. 8.

24. Thomas Gladwin, "Strategies in Delinquency Prevention," *Social Action and Reaction* (book presented for publication), p. 267. Dr. Gladwin is an anthropologist employed by the National Institute of Mental Health.

25. LaMar T. Empey and Jerome Rabow, "The Provo Experiment in Delinquency Rehabilitation," *American Sociological Review,* XXVI, No. 5 (Oct., 1961), 679-96. Recent analysis of data from the Provo program indicates an unexpectedly positive impact of the experimental intervention on the school performance of the subjects.

26. Frederick W. Englund, "A Report on Employment and Education Program for High School Dropouts" (presented to the Subcommittee on Employment and Manpower of the Committee on Labor and Welfare of the United States Senate, Aug. 6, 1963). Mr. Englund is divisional vice-president, Carson, Pirie Scott & Co., Chicago, Ill.

27. S. M. Miller, "Strategy, Structure, and Values in School Programs" (mimeographed paper, 1963), p. 7. Dr. Miller is a faculty member at the Youth Development Center, Syracuse University, Syracuse, N.Y.

28. Laurence Wylie, "Youth in France and the United States," *Daedalus,* Journal of the American Academy of Arts and Sciences (Winter, 1962), p. 206.

29. E. K. Nelson, Jr., "The Feedback of Research Information as a Stimulus for the Development of a Delinquency Prevention Program," *op. cit.*

30. Douglas Grant, "Toward a Rational Approach to Culture Change" (paper presented August 26, 1963 in Los Angeles at the Annual Meeting of the Society for the Study of Social Problems). Mr. Grant is chief of research, California Department of Corrections, Sacramento, Calif.

31. LaMar T. Empey and Jerome Rabow, "The Provo Experiment in Delinquency Rehabilitation," *op. cit.*, p. 685.

32. Examples of recently established structures which will seek to coordinate diverse public and private programs and to develop and innovate approaches to youth problems are: (1) The Youth Opportunities Board of Greater Los Angeles, 601 Old Hall of Records, 220 North Broadway, Los Angeles 12, California; (2) The North Carolina Fund, Training Center on Youth Crime, The Institute of Government, University of North Carolina, Chapel Hill, N.C.

33. For an assertion that the latent vested interests of subsystems make for only token and highly transitory movements toward agency coordination in delinquency prevention activities see Walter B. Miller, "Inter-Institutional Conflict as a Major Impediment to Delinquency Prevention," *Human Organization*, XVII (Fall, 1958), 20; and E. K. Nelson, Jr., "Community Approaches to the Prevention of Crime and Delinquency—Some Research Leads" (Los Angeles: Youth Studies Center, University of Southern California, 1961), Working Paper No. 4, pp. 5-7.

34. Alvin W. Gouldner, "Reciprocity and Autonomy," *op. cit.*, p. 257.

35. John M. Pfiffner, "Needed: A Geo-Political Approach to Law Observance" (Los Angeles: Youth Studies Center, University of Southern California, January, 1964).

36. Alvin W. Gouldner, "The Norm of Reciprocity," *American Sociological Review* XXV, No. 2 (April, 1960), 161-78. For a discussion of trends indicating gradual increases in reciprocal arrangements among agencies dealing with social deviance, see E. K. Nelson, Jr., "Research and Related Activities in the Crime and Delinquency Field," *Crime and Delinquency* (accepted for publication in the October 1964 issue).

37. The Youth Studies Center currently is conducting both basic research and community experimentation relative to the phenomena of inter-organizational conflict and accommodation in programs of youth.

3

ADMINISTRATIVE STYLES AND COMMUNITY LINKAGES OF PUBLIC SCHOOLS

SOME THEORETICAL CONSIDERATIONS *

Eugene Litwak and Henry J. Meyer

§   Introduction

In this paper we wish to consider the relationship between different social structures of schools and some procedures for linking schools to the outer community. We will limit consideration to individual schools (what practicing schoolmen call "the building") and exclude questions that might be raised by taking the total school system as the object of analysis. Furthermore, we examine those relation-

* Ideas advanced in this paper were developed in close collaboration with staff members of the Great Cities School Improvement Project of the Detroit Public Schools. We especially acknowledge the contributions of Carl Marburger and William Rasschaert. Many of the ideas are common currency among students of the sociology of formal organizations and we have not attempted exhaustive recognition of stimulation from such

ships that schools have with the families and neighborhoods containing their children rather than relations between schools and other local social institutions, such as law-enforcement agencies, economic enterprises, churches, welfare and social agencies. Thus, we wish to look at schools in their most proximate community relations. Our general point is that the nature of linkages between schools and families and neighborhoods affects the behavior of school children; and that variations in such linkages are affected by the social organization and administrative style of the schools.

Research bearing on this point is in progress but we will not report data here. More than three years of close observation of schools in Detroit and close association there with thoughtful educators who have been involved in programs of school-community relations will, we hope, provide empirical restraint. Our discussion will, however, be abstract and incomplete. We have sought to simplify the issues by generalizing them, fully aware of the difficulties of testing the theories and of translating them into operating programs.

In the sections of the paper we undertake the following: describe briefly some general positions on school-community relations; point out varieties of bureaucratic forms and administrative styles that appear to characterize schools; suggest a theoretical basis for evaluating these forms; propose a theory of linking mechanisms and a catalogue of such mechanisms evaluated by the theory; suggest a principle of optimal combination of school bureaucratic form

sources or from discussions with our colleagues, particularly Robert D. Vinter, and from our students at the University of Michigan. We wish also to acknowledge financial support from the U.S. Office of Education and from the President's Committee on Juvenile Delinquency and Youth Crime.

and linking mechanisms; and finally, suggest the combination that appears to us to be the most fruitful avenue to pursue to maximize desired school-community relations for purposes of effecting educational and social objectives.

§   Three Approaches to School-Community Relations

There are at least three major approaches to school-community relations, each with a reasonable claim to effective results for educational objectives. These can be roughly characterized as the "locked door," "open door," and "balance theory" (or shall we say "swinging door!") viewpoints.

"Locked Door"

The "locked door" position basically assumes that the schools can handle within their walls all major problems of education. Therefore, outer community participation should be kept to a minimum. The presence of parents in the school will hamper the professional educator in the performance of his duties. Lacking professional training and having strong emotional ties to the child, the parent will inhibit the use of professional judgment. This approach is consistent with some sociological theories that have dealt with relationships between large-scale bureaucratic organizations and family and neighborhood groups. Thus Weber points out that strong family systems tend to undermine the development of rational bureaucracies based on merit. Parsons implies that families and large-scale bureaucracies must be kept apart if each is to operate efficiently.[1] In practice, this approach is perhaps well illustrated in the French and German school systems. The question of interest here is "What bureaucractic forms and what linking procedures will keep the school and community at maximum social distance?"

"Open Door"

In direct contrast is the "open door" policy. The assumption here is that many of the basic educational processes take place outside the school building, in the family, peer group, and neighborhood. Furthermore, to generate educational motivation the educational experience must be related closely to the everyday life of the child. This necessitates very intimate school-community contacts. Although few sociological theories have expounded this approach, practitioners in many fields are actually working to induce closer contacts.[2] Most major cities have programs attempting to increase contact between schools and families. In one extreme example a school system has installed washing machines and cooking facilities so that families in need might use school facilities for their everyday living needs.

Again the question arises as to what bureaucratic forms and linking procedures will most likely produce this close contact with the community.

Balance Theory of Coordination

The balance theory of coordination accepts some validity in both the "open" and "locked door" approaches. It asserts that intimate and distant school-community relations must be balanced in different degrees under different circumstances to optimize effective educational objectives. This approach notes two kinds of errors into which a school-community program can fall. First, it can bring the schools and community so close together that professional standards are seriously weakened. Second, it can keep families and schools so far apart that lack of coordination permits contradictory influences to emanate from both sides. To avoid these errors the balance theory argues that optimal social distance is a determinable point between the extremes of intimacy and isolation. At such a point the schools will be close enough to coordinate behavior with the families but not so close as to disrupt the performance of professional educational tasks. This approach has been recently elaborated as a general theory of the effects of relationships between bureaucratic organizations and external primary groups on social control.[3]

It is important to note that the balance-theory approach implies that the extent of linkage between schools and the outer community should depend on whether the social distance is too close or too far. For example, a school might have a majority of southern rural migrant parents who are suspicious of the school and do not see the value of education. Another school in the same system might have a majority of parents from professional occupations who put excessive emphasis on education, scrutinize the school with microscopic care, and intrude in actions of the teachers. Still another school might have parents of both these kinds. In the first case, the balance-theory approach would suggest the need for linking procedures to close the distance, in the second case to increase social distance, and the third case would require the operation of both types of program. Under this approach, what bureaucratic forms and linking procedures can produce the desired balance implied by these three examples?

§   Concepts of Administrative Styles of Bureaucratic Structures

We recognize that the concept of "administrative style" of a school usually implies the form of management or leadership exercised by the principal. We use the term here, however, in the more general sense to refer to the total bureaucratic structure of the school without considering the extent to which this structure depends on the way the principal fills his role or the extent to which the principal's role is defined by other structural aspects of the school as a social organization.[4]

Are there some common bases which can be used to describe administrative styles which will encompass most empirical situations and which can then be used to show how administrative style is systematically linked to outer community relations? A review of the literature indicates a large number of concepts used to describe administrative style. Thus some students refer to process-oriented versus goals-oriented organizations;[5] others refer to the democratic, the autocratic and the laissez-faire;[6] others use terms like rationalistic or human relations; some use the terms bureaucratic and non-bureacratic;[7] and some differentiate between therapeutic versus custodial styles of organization.[8]

Basic Dimensions of Organizational Style

Seeking basic dimensions of administrative style, one could well argue that these different emphases all in fact deal with the same underlying issues.[9] This is exemplified by the classic features of bureaucracy as described by Max Weber, whose analysis may be summarized as involving consideration of the following:[10]

1. Authority structure—hierarchical or collegial
2. Division of labor—specialization or generalization
3. Interpersonal relations—impersonal or personalized relations
4. Performance guides—delimited, a priori rules; or internalization of organizational goals; or *ad hoc* determination of duties

5. Goal or policy setting—separation or merger of policy and administrative decisions
6. Personnel assignment—on basis of merit or on bases irrelevant to organizational goals

Descriptions of Types of Administrative Styles

The administrative style that Weber called "monocratic bureaucracy" can be described on these dimensions as follows: hierarchical authority, specialization, impersonal relations, a priori rules, separation of policy and administration, personnel assignment on basis of merit. This same characterization can be used as well to describe custodial emphasis in treatment organizations, the traditional form of German and French school organization, "scientific management" in industry, and what Simon has called "process" styles of administration. It is also suggestive of what some have called an "autocratic" group atmosphere.

If organizations are characterized by opposite poles of these dimensions (except personnel assignment) we find: collegial relations, generalization in division of labor, personalized relations, internalized organizational goals, merged policy and administrative decisions—and personnel assignment on basis of merit. Such an organizational style in industrial research has been called "human relations"; in education it has been associated with "progressive education"; in treatment organizations it suggests "therapeutic milieu"; it resembles what Simon calls the "goal-oriented" administrative approach; and it suggests what is sometimes implied by "democratic" group atmosphere.

These two administrative styles seem to represent opposites, stressing contrasting poles of each dimension except that of personnel assignment on the basis of merit. We have used the terminology of *rationalistic* and *human relations* styles respectively to refer to them. Both seem to be empirically visible among public schools. But this does not exhaust either the logical or the empirical types that result from variations in position on the basic dimensions.

Another administrative style seems particularly pertinent to educational organizations. It combines features of both rationalistic and human-relations styles, side by side in the same organization. In schools, scheduling of classes, fixing of hours devoted to subjects, keeping attendance and grade records, building maintenance, etc., seem to be run on a rationalistic basis, whereas classroom teaching, motivation and management of individuals and groups of children, communication and relations between teachers, etc. may be characterized by a human-relations style. Similar examples of such a mixed administrative style can be seen in hospitals, in colleges and universities, in large law firms, in industry, and elsewhere. We have called it *professional* administrative style because it so often highlights the relationship between professional personnel and the organization. One may argue that most organizations to some degree take this form, but some organizations, it seems to us, are exceptionally characterized in this way.

Organizations incorporating what may appear to be such contradictory rationalistic and human-relations elements can—and usually do—develop internal mechanisms to contain or isolate them although they often fail to eliminate all sources of internal strain. The analysis of such mechanisms is important but relatively neglected in theory and research; they cannot be derived from a consideration of either of the styles that seem together to characterize this bureaucratic form nor from the concept of an organizational continuum. They are distinctive to the professional administrative style. From preliminary analysis, it can be pointed out that the mechanisms include differential assignment of persons to roles, serialization of role performers within the same persons, temporal and spatial segregation of role performance, translator and other communication roles, evaluation groups, and other arrangements.

It is possible, in theory, to derive many other types of administrative style by varying these basic dimensions, but we shall not indulge in this logical exercise here. We note three such variations, however, that appear commonly in our observations of public schools. The first two are associated with rationalistic organizational form.

The *autocratic* administrative style has the attributes of the rationalistic organization except that a priori rules do not restrain and delimit the duties, powers, and privileges of superordinates, especially—in the school—those of the principal. Hence, the executive of the organization has considerable power to define areas of legitimate occupational endeavor in an arbitrary, and often personal, manner. This discussion ignores sources of restraint, other than those of the immediate organization, that might arise from the larger system—for example, the location of the principal in the total school system—or from other sources such as the subculture or social class of the population served.

The *paternalistic* administrative style—the variant of the rationalistic administrative style—reverses two of the dimensions: it does not have a priori delimitations of duties, especially executive duties; and it adopts personalized rather than impersonal relations between organizational members. The executive of the organization, the principal, may often appear genuinely concerned with his staff as persons and their performance; however, as in the autocratic type, arbitrary power remains with the superordinate to define the work situation and task assignments.

Both administrative styles tend to put the full burden

of decision making and the determination of merit on the executive, often on one man, such as the principal of the school. No organizational guarantees deriving from other members of the organization provide support for legitimate organizational goals. Such centralization of decision making may well lead to clogged communication channels and retarded decision processes. On the other hand, these administrative styles may function efficiently and effectively when the executive is able, has integrity, and is strongly committed to organizational goals consonant with those of the other members of the organization. In the school system, the concept of the principal as the "captain of his ship" is close to what is implied by both of these administrative styles.

A third type of bureaucratic form is a variant of the human-relations administrative style. We call it *laissez faire*. It is like the human-relations style except that performance determinants are neither a priori nor internalized but rather individualized on an *ad hoc* basis. As a consequence, members of the organization may make contradictory, uncoordinated determinations both of goals and of performance duties. One teacher might stress drill, another life experiences. Having a generally decentralized system of goal determination and of authority, and utilizing personalized relationships between members of the organization, the laissez faire bureaucratic form may well result in scattered islands of efforts. Some teachers may be successful and others not, but the school as an organization is unlikely, we hypothesize, to have or to achieve organizational objectives. This situation sometimes obtains during the pre-retirement years of a principal who has "given up" and whose school has previously taken the form of an autocratic, paternalistic, or even rationalistic administrative style.

All the types of administrative styles that have been described in this partial catalogue have been assumed to share in common the principle of assignment of personnel on the basis of merit. That is, organizational goals are the *desiderata* for appointment, training, promotion, elimination of members, evaluation in terms of monetary and other rewards. All the types are subject, however, to possible abandonment of this principle and might then be reasonably designated by such hyphenated terms as: rationalistic-non-merit, human relations-non-merit, paternalistic-non-merit, etc. The first three described above (rationalistic, human relations, and professional) would seem less likely than the last three (autocratic, paternalistic, laissez faire) to abandon the merit principle. In Table 1, where we summarize the features of these types of administrative style, we have suggested this likelihood by noting both merit and non-merit as characterizing the latter three.

It is sometimes assumed that adherence to the merit principle is synonymous with efficiency in the organization and effectiveness in achieving its goals whereas the absence of the merit principle produces the opposite. Although this seems plausible, we would not prejudge this empirical question. We have, however, tentatively accepted this position in our subsequent analysis.

Although any administrative style is subject to restatement in terms of the non-merit characterization of the dimension concerned with assignment of personnel, a pervasive infusion of non-merit criteria may produce, as we observe it, a distinctive enough form to justify special designation. This administrative style we call *nepotistic*, although the term is not entirely apt. Selected and rewarded regardless of performance on bases irrelevant to the achievement of organizational goals, personnel are members of the or-

Table 1—Administrative Styles as Defined by Dimensions of Organizational Structure

ADMINISTRATIVE STYLE

Dimensions of Organizational Structure	Rationalistic	Human-relations	Professional	Autocratic	Paternalistic	Laissez-faire	Nepotistic
Authority structure	hierarchy	collegial	hierarchy and collegial	hierarchy	hierarchy	collegial	Any combination of dimensions
Division of labor	specialization	generalization	generalization and specialization	specialization	specialization	generalization	
Interpersonal relations	impersonal	personal	impersonal and personal	impersonal	personal	personal	
Performance guides	a priori rules	internalized goals	a priori rules and internalized goals	ad hoc rules	ad hoc rules	ad hoc rules	
Goal or policy setting	separation of policy and administrative decisions	merger of policy and administrative decisions	both merger and separation of policy and administrative decisions	separation of policy and administrative decisions	separation of policy and administrative decisions	merger of policy and administrative decisions	
Internal mechanisms of isolation	none	none	present	none	none	none	
Personnel assignment	merit	merit	merit	merit and non-merit	merit and non-merit	merit and non-merit	non-merit

ganization because of personal or status considerations such as friendship, race, religion, social class, etc. Since organizational objectives have not governed their membership, benefits of the job may take precedence over performance. Some school administrators have called teachers with such orientations "mercenaries": they have given up (or never had) educational goals and are only interested in the money they earn. Principals, too, sometimes are so oriented. When this pervades the school, decisions and task performances are likely to reflect personal conveinence, which will usually, we hypothesize, not be identical with effective education.

Although we have discussed administrative styles without specific attention to children as members of the organization, their place obviously is affected by the particular style characterizing their school. Without developing this point, we note that when applied to children, non-merit styles may reflect conscious or inadvertent race and class biases both in educational materials and teaching styles as well as in evaluations of abilities and student achievement.

We will rest with the preceding crude delineations of administrative styles. Other styles are readily conceivable and some are empirically observable. Some types in particular are intermediate and transitional to those described. One obvious task for organizational research in the public schools is to determine whether these types, or others, account for the variations in school social organization that actually occur. We believe that a limited number of types reasonably reflect the empirical situation. On that assumption we turn next to the question: "Can we establish a basis for choosing among these administrative styles in the interest of achieving a balance in school-community relations?"

§   Criteria for Evaluating Administrative Style

We would like to elaborate one theory for assessing effectiveness of organizational form and to attempt applying it specifically to schools.[11] This will be done by taking the major dimensions of organization (e.g., hierarchy or collegial authority, impersonalized or personalized relations) and indicating under what conditions they might lead to effective organizational action. Once done, this should provide some basis for estimating how effective any given administrative style will be in accomplishing a given goal.

Hierarchy vs. Collegial Authority

In a large organization there must be some decision process available so that all members of the organization will have a common guideline. Where tasks are essentially repetitive and unambiguous, centralized a priori rules can provide this guideline. But where tasks or situations requiring action are not repetitive or when they are ambiguous, rules cannot be set up ahead of time or there may be no satisfactory way to make rules. Under these circumstances, some other system of authority must be provided to insure that decisions will be made and accepted. Some sort of authority structure seems to be necessary for coordination in a large organization.

Several assumptions are involved in the foregoing analysis. The first is that ambiguity about what can be done is not so great as to preclude all anticipation of decisions either by rules or policies. If this assumption did not hold, all decisions in a large organization would have to be passed to the top of the structure or to the collegium, and a vast overload would occur with inordinate delays (e.g., red tape) at the point of decision making. The second assumption is that those responsible for making decisions will be competent, by virtue of training or experience, to make the decisions. In a hierarchical authority structure if, in fact, people at the top could not make such decisions better than those at the bottom, the organization would not have the best possible direction; in a collegial authority structure if, in fact, given individuals rather than the collegium possess the competence, the organization is likewise deprived of the best decisions. (It is under these latter circumstances that the principle of "first among equals" appears to operate.) For either system of authority, a third assumption obtains: that the nature and variety of tasks are sufficiently limited so that persons at the top of the hierarchy or those composing the collegium can possess the necessary competence to make appropriate decisions. If, in fact, the organization faces many tasks for each of which different types of expertness is required, multiple hierarchies or collegia may be required.

We shall use the concept of "uniform" and "non-uniform" tasks or situations to refer to the issues involved in all these assumptions.[12] Where an organization must face many types of tasks or many ambiguous situations we shall say that it has "non-uniform tasks" and shall argue that hierarchical-authority structures have especially limited effectiveness. The effectiveness of one authority structure over another is a relative matter; it is, in the end, an empirical question.

When faced with non-uniform situations, collegial structure has some obvious advantages over hierarchical structure. For example, the collegium can assign to each member the responsibility most appropriate to his special competence. Thus the organization can approach the ideal of permitting the most expert persons in the organization to make decisions for the organization. But collegial structures have some equally obvious disadvantages: much communication is required and the time necessary to reach decisions is relatively long. Where there are predominately uniform tasks, or relatively few decisions to be made, a more or less permanent authority hierarchy is likely to be more efficient in reaching effective decisions.[13]

Specialization vs. Generalization in the Division of Labor

In an organization the virtues of specialization are obvious: a person can become more knowledgeable and skillful from practice when he does one job rather than many. However, there are circumstances when specialization is less virtuous! Where the task is constantly changing or not well standardized, specialization may be dysfunctional because the specialist may be trained for an obsolete task. Or, his training may become obsolete as the state of knowledge about the task changes. This is not merely a matter of wasted resources; frequently the specialist persists in using his obsolete specialized expertness so as to block progress to new skills. In short, a specialization may become a vested interest.[14]

What the generalist lacks of the specialist's expertness he gains presumably in acquiring principles applicable to various tasks. The risk of dilettantism, of being a "jack of all trades," is compensated for by adaptability to changing tasks and new skills and knowledge. It is noteworthy that progression up the administrative ladder in hierarchical organizations is accompanied by increasing generality of skill and knowledge, of transferability, and of responsibility for a wider range of decision making. In part, this is a function of job demands at higher levels where decisions must be made about many different operations and about their co-ordination, and where ambiguities and uncertainties about these decisions are more frequent. In general, as the tasks become less uniform, specialization becomes less useful and generalization more desirable.

Impersonal vs. Personalized Relations

The value of impersonal relations between members of a bureaucratic organization, according to some students of bureaucracy, rests in protection of rationality against extraneous personal demands, such as friendship, especially in such matters as evaluation of work and devotion to functional tasks. There is some evidence, however, that in situations of ambiguity individuals need personalized support if they are to work efficiently. Thus Blau points out that where individuals could not assess what was the right decision they confided in other members of their group who could understand their uncertainty without using it to evaluate them invidiously.[15] Others have held that where interpersonal skills are intrinsic in the job—as in combat teams in warfare, or psychotherapeutic treatment—personalized relations are necessary.[16] Such relations are exposed to the risk of irrationality (e.g., favoritism, nepotism), which may in part be avoided by internalization of the concept of merit, or by seeking some objective measure of output, or by separating evaluation from administration.

We would argue that from the viewpoint of administrative effectiveness the maintenance of impersonal relations would be desirable where there are relatively uniform tasks but that it would be less effective where the organization faces non-uniform and ambiguous situations.

Max Weber's analysis of bureaucracy noted the necessity of a priori rules that, among other effects, delimited duties and privileges of individuals in organizations. This facilitates coordination as well as specialization: for example, where standardized decisions can be anticipated by rules minimal demands are made on hierarchical decision making or personalized adaptability. The presupposition for this argument is, however, a preponderance of uniform tasks. Where tasks are non-uniform, they cannot be governed by a priori rules, for the rules would need to be too numerous to remember, would risk inappropriate application, or would overload the hierarchy of authority.

In non-uniform situations one alternative is to encourage internalization of general policies at all administrative and operational levels of the organization. When confronted by unanticipated or ambiguous events, members of the organization can then make judgments based on their understanding of organizational policy, goals, and values. The difficulty with such a solution to the problem of coordinating behavior is that means to achieve internalization of goals and policies are uncertain and those now available require stability of personnel and considerable investment of time and effort. Professions like social work and medicine, which involve many non-uniform tasks where a priori rules cannot be relied on, require long and expensive training and socialization before internalization of necessary principles (policies) can be assumed. In contrast, for the relatively uniform tasks of automobile assembly such lengthy processes would be unnecessary, as well as exorbitantly expensive.

An alternative to a priori rules and to internalization

of policies is the expediency of *ad hoc* determinations of duties as situations arise. In effect, this leaves the decision to the best judgment of members of the organization. If this judgment is guided by policy or organizational precedent, it is tantamount to internalization of policy; if it has no guide at all or only that of idiosyncratic experience, it can lead to organizational anarchy. It is most obviously useful when goals and values are well understood and accepted but when neither rules nor policies can be established. This can occur in new organizations, or for new directions in old organizations where goals are known but means are uncertain. In these circumstances it is useful or necessary to give individuals wide discretion. This is typically the arrangement in organizations of professionals, such as law firms and group medical practice, or when professionals are located within organizations to practice their professions. Thus, a street-gang worker employed by a community organization agency has few specific rules to follow in gaining the trust of a delinquent gang and redirecting their activity; the process is professional if not artistic, and he must make decisions and adaptations as he proceeds. Similarly, the psychotherapist can seldom be governed by a priori rules; his tasks are too ambiguous and his technology too uncertain. In such circumstances *ad hoc* determination of duties guided by general internalized policies may be the only reasonable arrangement. The risks are, of course, large; in particular, there are minimal bases for organizational evaluation of judgment and performance.

In general, a priori rules are most useful when the organization is faced primarily with uniform tasks. Internalization of policies and *ad hoc* determination of duties are preferable, or necessary, when the organization faces primarily non-uniform and ambiguous situations.

Separation vs. Merger of Policy and Administrative Decisions

To deal with changing demands on the organization as a whole, Max Weber concluded that effective bureaucracies must separate goal setting, or organizational policy, and administrative structures. What the organization *should* do was to be established by top management; administration consisted of those decisions which best implemented given policy. The previous line of reasoning should make our conclusion clear: such a separation is most effective when organizational tasks are primarily uniform. When the organization faces non-uniform tasks, goal setting and goal implementation through administrative decisions would seem to be more effective if they are merged.

Merit vs. Non-merit Evaluation of Personnel

All organizations must have criteria as well as having procedures for evaluating personnel. Evaluation is intrinsic in processes of recruitment, training and socialization, assignment to jobs, providing monetary and other rewards. Evaluation is implicated in the motivational system of the organization as well as in its system of membership maintenance. Effective organizations must require personnel evaluation to be based on performance in terms of organizational tasks and goals. This is the definition we give to "merit" as a basis for evaluation.

The use of non-merit, i.e., organizationally irrelevant, bases for evaluation of personnel is risky, for the results may or may not reduce organizational effectiveness. Nepotistic recruitment, for example, is an uncertain organizational principle, even though the boss's son may on occasion be the best man for the job.

Problems with the merit principle arise not from its

desirability but from its application. What criteria of merit can be applied? Without developing the argument here, we suggest that when the organization primarily faces uniform tasks, adherence to rules and policies is a meaningful criterion of merit. For organizations that deal with ambiguous tasks, however, such a criterion is less applicable or not applicable at all. In this situation, merit can be assessed only in terms of output or outcome variables. Where these are themselves uncertain, as they often are in education, treatment, and social service organizations, adherence to a preferred ideology within the organization is often substituted.[17] But this is a poor substitute criterion and often, in effect, constitutes non-merit evaluation.

SUMMARY OF BASES FOR EVALUATING ADMINISTRATIVE STYLES

Accepting the foregoing analysis of dimensions of bureaucratic organization, it is fairly obvious how the types of administrative style described earlier can be evaluated. The human-relations type would seem to be the best style when organizational tasks are non-uniform and ambiguous. The rationalistic style operates best when tasks are relatively uniform. The professional model is most suitable when both uniform and non-uniform tasks face the organization. Administrative styles accepting non-merit personnel assignments are likely to be less effective than those based on merit. We would expect autocratic and paternalistic styles to work better when there are uniform tasks and to work less effectively when tasks are non-uniform. The laissez-faire style, if it is effective at all, should work better for non-uniform situations. We cannot conceive of situations where the nepotistic administrative style would *necessarily* work effectively.

§   Administrative Styles vis-à-vis the Schools

Which administrative styles are best for public schools? This question can be entertained only if we add to the previous analysis certain assumptions. For example, empirical research is necessary to determine the uniform and non-uniform nature of school tasks, the character and clarity of school goals, the limits of school organizational flexibility. In addition, empirical examination of organizational effectiveness—the output of the schools—must be undertaken if a theory is to relate administrative style and effectiveness. Thus, to pursue our analysis we must make the necessary assumptions and utilize the criteria amplified above.

The "three R's" approach to education implies that the eduactional process consists basically of fairly uniform tasks. It assumes that children have fixed IQ's and that ways of motivating them are standard. Drill with predetermined materials is the pedagogical task, and standardized examinations assess academic achievement. Non-pedagogical tasks of the teacher and of the complement of school personnel fall into comparable uniform patterns.

In contrast, the "progressive education" approach argues that the chief problem is motivation and hence is highly individualized. In order to learn, the child must tie his individual experiences to the learning situation, which in turn must be tailored to each child. Hence, teaching styles and materials must be highly flexible to meet varied and changing abilities. No single standard of achievement is meaningful; motivation and growth cannot be reduced to common scores.

Of these exaggerated characterizations, of the three R and progressive education approaches, the first consists obviously of uniform tasks, for which our analysis prescribes a rationalistic administrative style. The second requires a human-relations style to deal with its extremely non-uniform tasks. Whether these extremes are ever to be found in fact and whether maximum effectiveness is achieved by the theoretically congruent administrative styles are, of course, matters for empirical determination. Casual observation suggests that even though these characterizations are a-typical they may be approximated.

More plausible, however, is the supposition that educational and socialization tasks of the public schools are both uniform and non-uniform. Not only are the housekeeping aspects of the school likely to be amenable to routine but so also are certain educational aspects. Thus, scheduling and distribution of time, some common evaluation standards, and even some teaching techniques may be conceived as uniform tasks. In fact, rules to guide performance as well as developed technology constantly convert non-uniform into uniform tasks. On the other hand, schools must still deal with motivation and socialization problems, though, which are not uniform. Moreover, the art of teaching and the organizational achievement of education demand far more than science and technology can now predict and standardize. Thus this is the condition for which our analysis asserts the appropriateness of the professional administrative style. It permits rationalistic management of the routine tasks of teachers and other persons in the organization while providing a human-relations style for non-uniform tasks. In a sense, this is the meaning of the assertion that the administrative style should allow the teacher to act as a professional.

As indicated earlier, a professional administrative style requires internal mechanisms to manage the potential conflict between rationalistic and human-relations components. The teacher as well as the organization must be protected against accepting either extreme as an exclusive approach. If, for example, the teacher is (or thinks he is) required to emphasize clerical and other routine aspects of the job, this emphasis may well pervade classroom teaching so that order and control take precedence over learning and socialization. Orderly records, neat rooms and neat children, and adherence to schedule may displace adaptability to individual differences and variability in teaching techniques. On the other hand, total neglect of routine in the interest of variability may well make the management of some essential organizational tasks impossible. Our observation is that this dilemma is critical for the school as a social organization. Its resolution requires deliberate attention.

Although we suspect that the professional administrative style will be generally most appropriate for public schools, we are not unmindful of the fact that different emphases within this form are probably required for different age-grade levels in the present structure of school systems and perhaps also for different social-class backgrounds of present school populations. Secondary-school levels may tip the balance toward the rationalistic style because socialization is less central and knowledge transmission more capable of standardization. In elementary schools the balance tips toward the human-relations style. Similar reasoning would suggest that low-income populations, with less educational motivation brought by children to the school than in higher-income populations, would respond to greater emphasis on the human-relations style.

To sum up the discussion, Table 2 suggests the kinds of tasks for which each administrative style is deemed most suitable.

**Table 2—Compatibility of Administrative Style
with Organizational Tasks**

KINDS OF TASKS

Administrative Style	Uniform (The 3 R's Approach)	Non-uniform (Progressive Education Approach)	Both Uniform and Non-uniform
Merit:			
Rationalistic	very high	moderately low	moderately high
Human-relations	moderately low	very high	moderately high
Professional	moderately high	moderately high	very high
Merit and Non-merit:			
Autocratic	low	extremely low	very low
Paternalistic	very low	very low	very low
Laissez-faire	extremely low	very low	very low
Non-merit:			
Nepotistic	lowest	lowest	lowest

§   Theoretical Basis for Selecting Linking Mechanisms

Our task now is to note what in theory would constitute the basis for deciding how schools as social organizations can be linked to their communities. Accepting the three
positions on school-community relations noted at the beginning of this paper—the "open door," "locked door," and
"balance theory"—let's consider implications of each position
for a theory of linking mechanisms.

"Open Door" Position

This position requires linking mechanisms that will
bring the proximate community into the school. Shortening
the distance between communicators is a central problem
of contemporary communication theory, and we can draw

on it for theoretical guidance. As in communication theory, differential consideration must be given to those situations in which the community is assumed to be hostile to the school and those in which it is assumed to be friendly. The oversimplification of these assumptions is acknowledged, but it is justifiable as a beginning.

Because the "open door" position faces its greatest challenge with a hostile community, we shall consider the nature of linking mechanisms under this condition: *four* types of problems must be met, and each suggests to us another new dimension on which to appraise linking mechanisms.

1. *Selective Listening: Organizational Initiative*

In communication theory, this is the problem of gaining attention for the message, since the fact is established that persons selectively listen to communicated messages.[18] The school must persuade hostile parents and neighborhood groups to receive its communication. The mistrustful or defiant family cannot be assumed to read information sent home, to join the parent-teacher association and attend its meetings, to take advantage of offers of teacher-parent conferences, to come voluntarily to the school when the child has a problem, to participate willingly in other activities related to the school. The school, then, must take great organizational initiative to reach such families and groups. So in its repertory of linking mechanisms, there must be some permitting such initiative: Sending an invitation to join the PTA represents little organizational initiative; sending a teacher—or an attendance officer—to visit the family in their home represents great organizational initiative.

2. Selective Retention: Intensity of Communication

Even when confronted with a message, some persons do not always accept it nor do they always retain it, and sometives they distort it in keeping with prior attitudes.[19] To meet this problem, the school must have among its linking mechanisms those that permit intensity of communication. Casual contacts or written communications have less intensity than protracted face-to-face communications involving an element of trust.

3. Feedback and Authoritative Adaptation: Focused Expertise

Many studies have shown that feedback and authoritative adaptation of the message facilitate acceptance of the communication, espeically when the message is complex. The communicator must be in a position to correct any misunderstanding and to restate the message if it is to be successfully conveyed. Some communications from schools are simple, such as a notice of a meeting or changed time for lunch hour; many are quite complex, such as an educational philosophy or the rationale for a new grading system. The school must be in a position to bring the expert into a face-to-face relation with the group being reached. We call this face-to-face confrontation between group and expert "focused *expertise*." [20] Classes for parents on how children learn provide a high level of focused *expertise;* a school newspaper provides very little.

4. Scope

If communication is sought with large numbers of persons rather than with individuals or very small groups, a means of communication with wide scope is obviously preferred. Schools taking an "open door" position often need to reach many parents and members of their community, thus, both as a matter of economy and of objective—other things being equal—linking mechanisms with the widest scope must be available to the school. Mechanisms vary in scope: within the same time and resource limits, personal conferences of the principal with each parent cannot reach as many families as a message sent home with the children.

We have not attempted to itemize and expand on all the possible dimensions of communication to which attention might be given when examining mechanisms that may link schools and communities. We have suggested, instead, the four dimensions that have great importance as criteria. For example, to bring a reluctant community as close to the school as the "open door" position requires, we would expect high levels of organizational initiative, intensity of communication, and focused *expertise* to be useful, and wide scope desirable if attainable.

"Locked Door" Position

This position advocates increasing social distance, that is, reducing intimacy between the school and its community. We suggest that the same dimensions are applicable as for the "open door" position, but the emphasis must be placed on opposite poles. Thus, linking mechanisms using *minimal* organizational initiative, intensity, focused *expertise,* and scope would be preferred. This argument needs no amplification; it is apparent in the earlier reasoning, and illustrations come readily to mind. In general, minimal and formal communications will serve best to wall out the community and discourage those who approach the school on their own initiative.

This position holds that optimum social distance between school and community achieves greatest educational
effectiveness. Because existing balances vary between
schools, and within them for different families and segments
of the community, linking mechanisms must be able to reduce social distance in some circumstances and increase it
in others. Mechanisms varying on the previously discussed
dimensions must be used selectively.

The "balance theory" position puts a greater burden
on the school organization than do the other two positions.
The school must be in a position continually to diagnose
the situation and to select appropriate linking mechanisms
to affect the balance. The crude dichotomies used to discuss
the dimensions on which mechanisms may vary are patently
inadequate. Rather, what is required is a much more subtle
programming of school-community relations by selecting
and sequencing and combining the linking mechanisms.

In discussing theoretical bases of linking mechanisms
we treated school-community relations entirely from the
viewpoint of the school. Moreover, only in the assumption
of hostile or cooperative orientations on the part of members
of the community have we implied that there may be situations in which the community may wish to *alter* these relations and, indeed, may take "positions" with respect to
desirable school-community relations. Here, however, we
must at least allude to the possibility of resistance by the
school to changes in their relations with the outer community. Of course, dimensions involved in linking mechanisms *from* and *to* bureaucratic organizations are not entirely
symmetrical, but they are not entirely asymmetrical either.
How parents and "citizens," individually or collectively,

might affect schools in the interest of educational objectives may well become a major consideration for careful theory and research in the present period of concern with desegregation, low standards, dropouts, and delinquency. With our immediate interest in school administrative style and school-community relations we have chosen to develop the other side, assuming that schools in general wish to maximize educational objectives rather than to resist changes to that end. We are aware that this may not be an entirely tenable assumption.

§   Empirical Classification of Linking Mechanisms and Their Theoretical Properties

By examining practice literature, and particularly by observing schools and their planned or unplanned management of school-community relations, we have noted a number of linking mechanisms which we shall try to catalogue roughly in this section. At the same time, we shall try to evaluate them in terms of the theoretical dimensions developed in the preceding section. It should be apparent that such an evaluation depends not only on the properties of the mechanisms but also on the school-community relations.

Following are the eight linking mechanisms. We have given them empirically suggestive, rather than theoretically consistent, names.

Detached Worker

In this mechanism, a professional person enters the family or home territory of those to be influenced, and by developing a trusting, quasi-primary-group relationship seeks to affect their relationship with the organization. Most obvious illustrations of this mechanism are the "street worker" with delinquent gangs and the "aggressive case-work" of social agencies.[21] In part, however, the school-community agent developed within the experimental Great Cities School Improvement Project of the Detroit Public Schools performs in this manner. Teachers and principals who regularly visit their children's homes, school nurses and social workers, and other such personnel may also represent this approach.

In terms of our criteria, the detached-worker mechanism has highest organizational initiative, high intensity, highest focused *expertise*, and lowest scope. It is therefore very useful in supporting an "open door" position and undesirable for a "locked door" position on school-community relations. From a "balance theory" position, it can be useful especially as a first step in bridging extreme social distance between school and community; it would be both wasteful and counterindicated when school and community are already too close.

Opinion Leader

This mechanism uses indigenous leaders through whom the families and neighborhood are influenced in their relationship with the organization. This approach too, has been used in delinquency areas.[22] Unless opinion leaders are created rather than found, this mechanism permits little organizational initiative and provides little focused *expertise*, but it has high intensity and moderate scope. The "natural leader," by definition, has intense relations with those to be affected and presumably reaches them through a cumulative network. But he is not a professional person and his orientation toward the objectives of the organization is generally outside the control of the organization. Indeed, if he is to retain his leadership, he may be more responsive to the orientations of his followers than to those of the organization. This limits the mechanism when there is wholesale hostility to the organization; however, when only some families or groups are hostile the mechanism can be very effective.

Schools often use this mechanism, and some have deliberately cultivated it as part of the school-community agent's effort. Unless coupled with such a mechanism as the detached worker, the opinion-leader mechanism would not advance the objectives of the "open door" position in a hostile community. From a "locked door" position it might well have contrary effects unless, of course, it were used negatively, i.e., to discourage interest in the school. In a carefully diagnosed situation, the mechanism might be useful in achieving "balanced" position, but the key to its utility probably lies in coupling or sequencing it with other mechanisms. Its chief shortcoming when used alone with hostile groups is the relative absence of focused *expertise*, which may be crucial in the communication of complex information. It may be overintense and needlessly limited in scope when distance is to be increased.

Settlement House

This mechanism involves the provision of physical facilities and professionals located where those to be affected can make use of them. It is illustrated by some "community school" approaches where more is intended than merely to "open the school to the public after school hours." It presupposes purposeful use of professional personnel to influence those entering the facility.[23] It is therefore moderate to high in intensity but only moderate—somewhere between the detached-worker and opinion-leader mechanisms—in organizational initiative. Its potential for focused *expertise* as well as intensity is considerable, especially if programs of group experience are developed by professional persons. Lacking great organizational initiative, its scope depends on the attraction of voluntary participants unless it is coupled with mechanisms of more initiative. Used alone it is not likely to further an "open door" position in a hostile community; it is obviously counterindicated for the "locked door" position. Again, from the position of "balance theory," the utility of the settlement-house mechanism depends on which direction the balance is to be tipped and, except for the maintenance of an already optimal balance, would need to be coupled or sequenced with other mechanisms.

Voluntary Associations

A voluntary association involving members from both the organization and the community can be established as a linking mechanism. The most obvious illustrations of this mechanism are the parent-teacher associations and home-room mothers' clubs. The voluntary associations we have in mind, it should be understood, are subject at least partially to official organizational control and are not independent.

As a mechanism, the voluntary association has very little organizational initiative but must, like the settlement house, wait for the community to come to it, unless it is supplemented by another mechanism with more initiative, such as the detached worker. It is also moderate to low on intensity, since its primary contact is in periodic meetings. It can bring some, but not much, focused *expertise* to bear, inasmuch as presumably professional persons from the organization come into direct contact with persons from the community, but such contacts are usually formal or casual except for persons in active association roles. It can have rather wide scope since the voluntary organization can be as inclusive as its membership definition permits. If it is a parent-teacher association, it is limited to these membership classes, and hence its scope is restricted unless its meetings are open to others from the community.

From a "locked door" position on school-community relations, the voluntary association is a useful mechanism if any link is necessary. Operated formally, it can maintain or increase distance. For the "open door" position, this mechanism has limited utility when used alone; yet its scope recommends it when relations are already cooperative and need to be stabilized. From the "balance theory" position, the voluntary association is very useful if the population is identified with the school but not very useful if it is distant.

As a widely used linking mechanism in American public schools, the parent-teacher association often exhibits its defects under the contrasting situations of indifferent or suspicious parents in depressed areas and aggressively interested parents in the high-income suburbs. In the former, the PTA is often small and impotent, composed only of the few parents with initiative or willingness to acquiesce in appeals from the principal; the principal often sees his "problem with the PTA" as that of generating wider interest. In the suburbs, the PTA is often strong and large; the principal often sees his problem as one of containing its manifold invasions of the school. Obviously, it cannot be the universal linking mechanism for all schools.

Common Messenger

This mechanism uses members common to both the organization and the community groups to be affected as a messenger to link them. Sending messages home with the children is the most obvious example, and the use of parents as auxiliary school personnel is another example. As common members, they may communicate in both directions. This mechanism has a moderate amount of organizational initiative, since the school has constant contact with the family through the messenger; however, the unreliability of some messengers—such as children taking home school notices—is notorious. The common-messenger mechanism has moderate intensity by providing continuous membership in the primary groups. This intensity may, of course, be diluted by lack of interest or opposition from the messenger; it depends also on his effective position in either group. The mechanism has very little inherent focused *expertise;* in fact, the content of the communication—particularly that verbally conveyed—may well become distorted. But the mechanism has considerable scope, especially for the school, for it may reach all or most parents economically.

This mechanism can be used as an insulated form of communication by schools taking the "locked door" position; it is mediated, arms-length communication not likely to encourage close contact from the community; the school has a high degree of control over what is communicated. The mechanism would seem to be only supplemental to other mechanisms for schools taking the "open door" position; it cannot be confidently relied upon except as a first step toward greater involvement. Likewise, from a "balance theory" position the common-messenger mechanism is selectively useful in a sequence of mechanisms or as a complementary mechanism.

Mass Media

This formal mechanism, whose character is conveyed by its name, has moderate to low organizational initiative, since its capacity to reach persons depends on, for instance, their willingness to read the newspaper, turn on the radio, pause to see the poster in the grocery store. Techniques of saturation advertising, however, can provide some prospect of getting messages to their targets. Of all mechanisms so far discussed, mass media has the least intensity and minimal focused *expertise*. What it possesses to a high degree is scope.

It is a favored mechanism for the "locked door" position since it can give the semblance of communication without much risk of affecting those it reaches. For the same reason, it has limited utility as a major linking mechanism from the viewpoint of the "open door" position. Its utility from the viewpoint of a "balance theory" position will depend on which direction the balance is to be shifted: if distance is desired, it is useful; if intimacy, it has little usefulness.

Formal Authority

Public schools, like many other public organizations, are vested by law with types of authority that may serve as mechanisms for reaching members of the community. The attendance officer represents such a mechanism; so does the school official with authority to reject, suspend, or expel a student. With strong sanctions behind it, formal authority has high organizational initiative for it can usually deliver its message, a message however of specialized and limited objective. Although its power is likely to insure that the school's message is also heard, intensity, in the sense we have defined the dimension, is rather low for formal authority; it is not likely to generate trust and confidence and because of this, many helping professions dependent on intensive relationships (such as social casework) shy away from it. The formal-authority mechanism may bring considerable focused *expertise* to bear, but professional expertness, even when available, often is circumscribed by enforcement duties inherent in the role. The recent tendency to surround authoritarian roles with therapeutic objectives and techniques (the truant officer has become the attendance officer!) moves the potential of this mechanism toward that of the detached worker, but the ambiguity of such a new role definition is yet to be fully exposed and resolved. Formal authority in its symbolic sense is broad, since all subject to the authority may be made aware of the organization's expectations. But since it is embodied in enforcement personnel and since they are usually few in number, actual scope may not be very wide.[24]

With its limited intensity and its restricted content of communication formal authority is often useful from a "locked door" position, since it has the additional advantage of emphasizing the formal rather than the informal relations between school and community. For the same reasons, it is rejected from the "open door" position. It is probably more useful for increasing than for decreasing distance in the interests of a "balance theory" position. The modification of some aspects of this mechanism so as to take advantage of its strong organizational initiative is yet to be explored and may offer promising possibilities as a school-community link.

Delegated Function

This is not a linking mechanism in the same sense as the others. They contemplated communication essentially with primary groups in the community. By calling attention to delegation of function we recognize that the community also contains other organizations and associations and that the school can (and indeed must) link itself to them and through them to the community. Such organizations may facilitate or impede the school's objectives—but we will not develop this issue. We shall note only that in a number of circumstances schools often turn some of their functions over to other organizations: other organizations, such as physicians and medical facilities, may be more competent to perform the function: other organizations, such as churches, may have better access to people the school wishes to reach; other organizations, such as block clubs and political associations, may carry more influence and be willing to use it on behalf of school objectives. For these and other reasons, schools may seek to relate to the community through other organizations.

Some attention has been given elsewhere to the general problem of coordination between organizations, but further specific consideration of schools is needed.[25] To which organizations schools delegate functions and with what effects are still unexplored questions, but there are obvious differences between delegating school-ground behavior problems to the police and to a group-work agency. How other organizations can serve the schools as communications links is largely neglected as a problem for theory and research. It would seem likely, however, that in this process the organization to which some function is delegated would make use of the linking mechanisms discussed above.

We have prepared Table 3 to compare the various linking mechanisms roughly with one another on the dimensions

Table 3—Underlying Principles of Communication Related to Mechanisms of Coordination between Bureaucratic Organizations and External Primary Groups

PRINCIPLES OF COMMUNICATION

Coordinating Mechanisms:	Organizational Initiative	Intensity	Focused Expertise	Scope
Detached Expert	highest	high	highest	lowest
Opinion Leader	low	highest	low	moderate to low
Settlement House	moderate to low	high-moderate	high	moderate
Voluntary Associations	lowest	moderate-low	moderate	high to moderate
Common Messenger	moderate	moderate-low	lowest	highest
Mass Media	moderate to low	lowest	lowest	highest
Formal Authority	high	low	high to moderate	moderate
Delegated Function	high	high to low	high to low	moderate

considered. Table 4 summarizes how each of the positions on school-community relations might evaluate these mechanisms. Both comparisons are implicit in the previous discussions of the mechanisms.

Because they are empirical rather than theoretical, most of the mechanisms we have discussed present mixed properties. One potential value of attempting to state the underlying dimensions of linking mechanisms is the possibility of inventing new ones expressly designed for particular objectives of the school. We would not expect the empirical examples to exhaust the possibilities.

Table 4—Comparative Usefulness of Linking Mechanisms for Three Positions on School-Community Relations

Linking Mechanism	"Open Door" Position	"Locked Door" Position	"Balance Theory" Position
Detached worker	Very high	Very low	Very high when di is to be decreased when community i tile). Very low wh tance is to be inc (e.g., when com too involved).
Opinion Leader	Potentially moderate when community is friendly or when coupled with another mechanism (e.g., detached worker, mass media) used for recruitment.	Very low	Potentially moderate distance is to b creased through sity. Very low wh tance is to be inc
Settlement House	High. Potentially very high when community is friendly.	Very low	High when distance be decreased t focused expertise. low when distance be increased.
Voluntary Association	Moderate. Potentially very high when community is friendly.	Moderate	Moderate when dist to be decrease scope. Moderate distance is to creased.
Common Messenger	Low	High	Moderate when dist to be decrease scope. Moderate distance is to creased.
Mass Media	Low. Potentially high when community is friendly and when coupled with an intense mechanism.	High	Very low when dist to be decreased when distance is increased.
Formal Authority	Very low	Very high	Very low when dist to be decreased high when distan increased.

§ Relationship between Administrative Styles and
Linking Mechanisms

We are now in a position to consider how various
school administrative styles are related to different school-
community linking mechanisms. To do so we will briefly
state what we see as the organizational potential for consistency between linking mechanisms and administrative
style. By consistency we mean the extent to which both
linking mechanisms and administrative styles stress such
common dimensions as hierarchy or collegial relations, rules-
oriented or internalized values, impersonal or personal relations, etc. We here view linking mechanisms as based
partially within the organizational structure. If they stress
dimensions of work contradictory to the rest of the organization, internal friction will develop which will divert
energy from organizational goals. Given this underlying
assumption we then ask: "Which administrative styles are
capable of utilizing which linking mechanisms?" We suggest some hypotheses below, but information is so sparse
that much more empirical research is required before a
persuasive theory of consistency can be elaborated.

Some mechanisms are clearly more consistent with the
human-relations than with the rationalistic administrative
style. Thus the detached worker requires decentralized
rather than hierarchical authority, internalization of policy
rather than a priori rules, generalized rather than narrowly
specialized assignment of duties, merger of policy and administrative decisions, and probably personalized rather
than impersonal relations within the organization. Only the
human-relations administrative style, or its embodiment in
the professional style, could permit the autonomy, flexibility,

and adaptability required in the detached-worker role. These are inconsistent with rationalistic styles, whether merit or non-merit. In one instance a school-community agent seeking to act like a detached worker was prevented from doing so by the principal's requirement that he sign out and indicate precisely where and how long he would be in a predesignated place; he was also required to "clear" all plans for meeting with groups of parents and others in the community.

The settlement-house mechanism is similarly more consistent with a human-relations administrative style than with a rationalistic one, since it requires personalized relations and adaptability in task performance as well as in professional discretion. The opinion-leader mechanism would also appear more consistent with the human-relations than with the rationalistic style, since extra-organizational procedures may be desirable to reach opinion leaders with certain kinds of information, and these procedures are likely to develop in a less hierarchical, less rules-oriented structure. However, since the opinion leader may be a conveyor of information whatever its source, this mechanism may also be consistent with rationalistic structures when operating in conjunction with other mechanisms such as mass media.

In summary, we would say that human-relations organizational structures are particularly able to utilize the detached-worker, settlement-house, and probably opinion-leader linking mechanisms.

Some mechanisms are clearly more consistent with a rationalistic administrative style. Formal authority and mass media both lend themselves to hierarchical control and executive management, both tend to be impersonal, and neither conflicts with a priori definitions of organizational tasks or with specialized-job duties. We have already noted the possibility that the opinion-leader mechanism, also, is consistent with this administrative style.

The other mechanisms are not so easily assignable to human-relations or rationalistic administrative styles, and hence must be treated as available to either. *How* they are used would seem more affected by administrative style than *whether* they can readily be used. Thus, a parent-teacher association may be instituted and operated from the top of an authority hierarchy (and this is often the case) or from a more general impetus. The common-messenger mechanism lends itself to formal or informal use, under strict rules or general policy or wide discretion. The use of delegated function as a mechanism—referrals to agencies, invitations to organizations to work with the school, for example— would also seem to depend on how delegation was accomplished, what functions were delegated, and which other organizations were used. These might be affected by the organizational structure of the school as well as by its definition of goals and objectives, but any of the administrative styles we have identified would seem capable of using the mechanism.

Presumably the professional administrative style, containing both rationalistic and human-relations components, would have the widest range of linking mechanisms consistent with it. None of the mechanisms can be inconsistent with it, as they may be with other administrative styles; hence the internal organizational strains generated by inconsistent structures would be minimized.

Our speculations lead us to suggest the following ranking of combinations of administrative style and linking mechanisms in terms of their capacity to carry on school-community relations: The merit styles—rationalistic, human relations, and professional—utilizing consistent mechanisms will have the greatest capacity; next will rank rationalistic and human-relations styles but utilizing inconsistent mechanisms; below these will come the non-merit administrative styles varying in rank with the consistency of mechanisms utilized but with the laissez-faire structure probably ranking quite low. Nepotistic structure could not be consistent with any mechanisms and we would rank it lowest of all.

Which of these combinations is preferable is not merely a matter of presumed capacity to carry on school-community relations. A choice will also depend on the position taken on school-community relations. If one takes the "locked door" position, we would suppose that the rationalistic administrative style with consistent linking mechanisms would offer a positive combination. If a negative approach were proposed—that is, if the "locked door" is to be achieved by ineffective school-community relations efforts—the non-merit administrative styles with inconsistent mechanisms ought to satisfy this purpose. The professional administrative style utilizing distance-creating mechanisms ought to be another effective combination for deliberately achieving a "locked door" position. The human-relations style with consistent mechanisms would probably be least effective for this purpose.

If an "open door" position is intended, the selection of combinations should probably be the reverse of that just given, with the human-relations style and consistent mechanisms most promising, the combination with professional style next, and rationalistic styles and inconsistent and non-merit combinations last. Depending on the direction indicated for a "balance theory" position on school-community relations, a professional administrative style with combinations of mechanisms chosen in the interests of closing or increasing distance would undoubtedly be preferred. None

of the other combinations would permit either or both
directions to be pursued in the same program of school-
community relations.

§ Conclusion

The models of administrative styles, linking mechanisms, and their combinations that we have just sketched
from a theoretical perspective have been based on certain
simplifying assumptions about the nature of school social
organization, communication structures, objectives of school-
community relations, and the interrelationships of all of
these. We have tried to indicate our assumptions and the
reasons why we make them. Basically, we can only use our
best hunches until the evidence gives direction to more
convincing hypotheses.

Nor have we exhausted the possible models of school-
community relations that might be developed on our own
assumptions. One might imagine a school divided horizon-
tally with a rationalistic style between teachers and children
and a human-relations style among the staff and the school
taking a "locked door" position with respect to community
relations and utilizing distance-maintaining mechanisms. In
our terms this would, of course, be a professional administrative style, but it would differ from the one elaborated in
this paper. Or one might imagine a human-relations school
that has a "locked door" position vis-à-vis the community
and utilizes mechanisms to achieve the separation. Again,
this would in our terms represent another variant, probably
requiring some social organization resembling but nevertheless differing from the professional administrative style we
have described.

We have tried to describe forms that seem most common in our observations and most plausible in our thinking. Only empirical data can tell us what, in fact, are the relationships between administrative style, linking mechanisms, and school-community relations policies. We sense that there is some strain toward consistency between these aspects of the phenomenon we wish to understand. We suspect that the same factors that generate a human-relations administrative style, for example, predispose toward an "open school" position and create a tolerance for distance-closing linking mechanisms.

In the course of this paper we have tried to indicate some basic dimensions for analyzing school administrative styles (e.g., hierarchy, impersonality, specialization, etc.). Then we developed bureaucratic models using those dimensions (e.g., human relations, rationalistic, etc.). Next we suggested a principle for evaluating administrative styles in terms of the uniformity or non-uniformity of the tasks they must undertake.

We then turned to a discussion of linking mechanisms, identifying four principles which in theory seem basic to them (initiative, intensity, focused *expertise,* and scope). We attempted to catalogue eight empirically observed linking mechanisms and to analyze them in terms of their inherent properties. This permitted an assessment of the utility of these mechanisms for each of three positions taken toward school-community relations ("locked door," "open door," and "balance theory"). We then sought through a principle of consistency to suggest how our theories of administrative style and linking mechanisms might be combined. Finally, we tried to utilize the foregoing analysis to suggest combinations of administrative style and linking procedures which seem consonant with the three approaches to school-community relations.

The major import of this paper is that it seeks to tie together several bodies of theory and by so doing point out the paths where future knowledge must be gained. We hope that opening the discussion in this manner will stimulate further systematic thought and research, for clearly our statement is at best only an uncertain beginning in such an inquiry.

Notes

1. T. Parsons, *The Structure of Social Action* (New York: The Free Press, 1949), pp. 542-52; *The Theory of Social and Economic Organization,* translators A. M. Henderson and T. Parsons (New York: Oxford University Press, 1947), pp. 354-58; T. Parsons, "The Social ·Structure of the Family," *The Family: Its Function and Destiny,* ed. Ruth N. Anshen (New York: Harper & Row, Publishers, rev., 1959), pp. 260-63; George A. Theodorson, "Acceptance of Industrialization and Its Attendant Consequences for the Social Patterns of Non-Western Societies," *American Sociological Review,* XVIII (October, 1953), 480-81.

2. The revival of local organizing efforts of political parties— "volunteers," neighborhood units, clubs, and so on—seems evident, taking account of family and friends. In delinquency control efforts, there is growing recognition that delinquents cannot be treated as isolated individuals but must be reached through their significant primary groups, such as gangs. This has led to the development of street-gang programs such as those of the New York City Youth Board. In education there is also increasing concern with the need for closer relations between schools and families where there has been extensive breakdown in the educational process. Thus the Detroit and the Flint, Michigan, school systems have crystallized these trends into major programs to bring school and family closer together. In Detroit a special, new position has been created—the school-community agent—to facilitate this linkage in low-income areas, where educational efforts have had limited success. In fundraising endeavors the importance of grassroot, primary-group ties is recognized in the efforts of major health foundations to use local-

neighborhood residents to collect funds in their own neighborhoods. For a case study of how hospital and local-community volunteers coordinate their behavior to maximize goal achievement see Otto Von Mehring, "The Social Self-Renewal of the Mental Patient and the Volunteer Movement" in Milton Greenblatt, Daniel J. Levinson, and Richard Williams (eds.), *The Patient and the Mental Hospital* (New York: The Free Press, 1957), pp. 585-93.

3. Eugene Litwak and Henry J. Meyer, "A Balance Theory of Coordination Between Bureaucratic Organizations and External Primary Groups" (unpublished manuscript avilable in mimeograph).

4. Our observation has led us toward the conclusion of many public school educators: that the principal is, empirically, a key person in the school building, perhaps occupying *the* key position. The principal appears to have wide latitude in the translation of policy into practice and hence in defining goals and their implementation for his building. The principal is, of course, subject to the constraints of the larger school system—such as tenure and centralized assignment of teachers, system-wide curricular and other decisions, and centralized budget control. And he is limited, too, by the character and organization of his own staff, by traditions of classroom autonomy of teachers, by sex-role relationships, and so on. Nevertheless, how the principal carries out his role seems to account more than any other single factor *within* the school system for the observable variability of bureaucratic form among buildings. However, until further research has established the interplay of the principal and other elements, we shall conceive of the administrative style of the school, as in this paper, in terms of the total social structure.

5. James G. March and Herbert A. Simon, *Organizations* (New York: John Wiley & Sons, Inc., 1958), p. 29.

6. Most of these stem from the discussion by Ronald Lippitt and Ralph White. See *Group Dynamics: Research and Theory*, eds. D. Cartwright and A. Zander (2nd ed.; New York: Harper & Row, publishers, 1960), pp. 527-53.

7. *From Max Weber: Essays in Sociology*, trans. and eds. H. H. Gerth and C. Wright Mills (New York: Oxford University Press, 1946), pp. 196-203.

8. M. Greenblatt, "Implications for Psychiatry and Hospital Practice: The Movement from Custodial Hospital to Therapeutic

Community," in M. Greenblatt *et al.* (eds.), *The Patient and the Mental Hospital* (New York: The Free Press, 1957), pp. 611-20.

9. The following discussion on administrative style is in part a summary and in part an elaboration of an article by Eugene Litwak, "Models of Bureaucracy Which Permit Conflict," *The American Journal of Sociology*, LXVII (September 1961), 177-84.

10. *From Max Weber* . . . , *op. cit.*, pp. 196-203.

11. This formulation is based on Litwak, "Models . . ." *op. cit.* However, there are other theories that might be used as well, such as James D. Thompson and Arthur Tuden, "Strategies, Structure, and Processes of Organizational Decision," in James D. Thompson *et al.* (eds.), *Comparative Studies in Administration* (Pittsburgh: Pittsburgh University Press, 1959), pp. 195-216; or Peter M. Blau and Richard W. Scott, *Formal Organizations* (San Francisco: Chandler Publishing Company, 1962), pp. 40-58.

12. We do not imply by this distinction that uniformity or non-uniformity necessarily inheres in the task, nor that tasks retain their character in this respect. Tasks may be "defined" by custom or fiat as uniform and hence treated as such in an organization; and technology for performing the task may be more or less standardized. Given complex and uncertain organizational goals, however, there may be classes of tasks that are intrinsically less likely than other tasks to be, or to become, "uniform."

13. For cases where hierarchy does not permit commitment to decisions, see March and Simon, *op. cit.*, p. 81.

14. For some of the weaknesses of specialization see Harold L. Wilensky and Charles N. Lebeaux, *Industrial Society and Social Welfare* (New York: Russell Sage Foundation, 1958), pp. 235-65. For an illustration of movement from specialization to generalization see R. A. Cohen, "Some Relations Between Staff Tensions and the Psychotherapeutic Process," in *The Patient and the Mental Hospital, op. cit.*, pp. 307-308.

15. Peter M. Blau, *Bureaucracy in Modern Society* (New York: Random House, Inc., 1956), pp. 63-4.

16. Edward A. Shils and Morris Janowitz point out that a sense of primary-group loyalty may be so strong among combat troops that it is given greater weight than the risk of death. See "Cohesion and Disintegration in the Wehrmacht in World War II," in Daniel

Katz *et al.* (eds.), *Public Opinion and Propaganda* (New York: The Dryden Press, Inc., 1954), pp. 91-108.

17. This point is discussed in reference to "people-changing organizations" by Robert D. Vinter, "Analysis of Treatment Organizations," *Social Work*, VIII (July, 1963), 14-15.

18. Herbert H. Hyman and Paul Sheatsley, "Some Reasons Why Information Campaigns Fail," *Public Opinion Quarterly*, XI (Fall, 1947), 412-23.

19. Hyman and Sheatsley, *loc. cit.*; Katz and Lazarsfeld, *op. cit.*, pp. 48-66; Eugene Litwak, "Some Policy Implications in Communications Theory with Emphasis on Group Factors," *Education for Social Work*, Proceedings, Seventh Annual Program Meeting (New York: Council on Social Work Education, 1959), pp. 97-101.

20. The advantages of focused *expertise*—or interpersonal relations—over mass media as a means of exerting influence are enhanced when encountering situations where complex messages must be transmitted. See P. F. Lazarsfeld, P. F. Berelson, and H. Gaudet, "The People's Choice" in William Petersen (ed.), *American Social Patterns* (New York: Doubleday & Company, Inc., 1956), pp. 164-69.

21. For a description of one such program see P. L. Crawford, D. I. Malamud, and J. R. Dumpson, *Working with Teenage Gangs*, Welfare Council of New York City, 1950.

22. S. Kobrin, "The Chicago Area Project: A Twenty-five Year Assessment," *Annals of the American Academy of Political and Social Sciences* (1959), Vol. 322, pp. 19-37.

23. L. T. Empey and J. Rabow, "The Provo Experiment in Delinquency Rehabilitation," *American Sociological Review*, XXVI (October, 1961), 679-95.

24. For a summary of thinking on the operation of law in social control, see the hypotheses suggested in F. James Davis *et al.*, *Society and the Law* (New York: The Free Press, 1962), pp. 88-90.

25. Eugene Litwak and Lydia F. Hylton, "Interorganizational Analysis: A Hypothesis on Coordinating Agencies," *Administrative Science Quarterly*, VI (March, 1962), 395-420.

4

THE YOUTH CULTURE, THE SCHOOL
SYSTEM, AND THE SOCIALIZATION
COMMUNITY

Ronald Lippitt

The paper is divided into two sections: the first summarizes the functions of the community and the school system as agencies and environments for youth development;
the second section summarizes and illustrates several courses
of youth-development action.

§ Diagnostic Observations

My conclusions and illustrations are drawn mainly from
our community programs of youth-development action research in Chicago, Illinois, and Flint, Michigan, from our
research relations with about a dozen elementary and secondary schools, and from the diagnostic and action research
of other investigators such as Reiss, Miller, Gross, Ohlin,
Cohen, and others.

One can describe and assess a community in various
dimensions: its political functioning, its economic stability,

or its physical plan and structure. I want to think of it in terms of its socialization design: its program for rearing, educating, assimilating the young. This is the area of activity which I term the "socialization community."

The Socialization Community

In studying a city of 200,000, we were able to differentiate seven community socialization functions ' carried on by professional socialization agencies and agents: (1) formal education, (2) religious development, (3) leisure-time recreation, (4) therapeutic and re-education services, (5) economic role-socialization, (6) political role-socialization, and (7) social control or legal-code socialization.

We found half-a-dozen community leaders who could nominate several persons in six of these areas. By asking each of the nominees to designate the most influential leaders in their area of socialization activity, we were able to identify, by a rank-ordering procedure among informants, about seventy influential leaders in these six areas. The one area which proved a vacuum was that of integrating the young into the political system of the community. Considerable disagreement arose as to who were the key leaders in economic-system socialization, because those training for occupational roles, those hiring youth, and those placing youth did not perceive and nominate each other consistently.

We interviewed the nominated leaders to get their conceptions of the socialization job, their conceptions of deviancy and its causes, and the amount of communication and of coordination of effort among themselves. From these two- or three-hour interviews, I shall present a few findings:

First, greater communication and perception of common goals occurred among leaders within the same socialization function than occurred among leaders across functions.

Much disagreement arose as to what was the most serious type of deviant development among the young in the community. The leaders were asked to regard the community as a producer of young people: What were good products and what were poor products of the community? The educators, the religious leaders, and the recreation directors stressed deviancy of social relations and lack of respect for adults. The economic-integration leaders stressed laziness, lack of work incentive, and disrespect for property. Therapeutic workers and legal-control officials stressed a lack of values and immaturity of impulse control.

When asked the causes of undesirable as well as desirable behavior, half the educators gave the family most credit for good outcomes; a third credited the school with most influence; others mentioned the church and the community.

When queried about the causes of bad behavior, three-quarters of the educators blamed the parents; the larger society, outside of the community, was mentioned next most frequently; school, church, or community were not mentioned as responsible for any bad effects.

The responses of leaders in other areas followed the same pattern, although the educators alone viewed the school as a potent cause of good behavior. Other leaders gave the community more credit for positive influence than did the educators.

The economic leaders placed more blame on the family: Ninety-two per cent of them cited the family as the major cause of deviant behavior.

Only the religious and leisure-time workers saw peers as a significant cause of deviancy.

The economic-socialization agents disagreed strongly with other leaders in believing that deviant behavior could be corrected by more discipline.

The religious and economic leaders felt that the major corrective action should be taken by the family.

The therapeutic agents considered individual counseling and guidance as needed most.

The educators expressed a broader perspective of need for individual counseling, involvement in new group activities, and action on changing the attitudes and organization of the community to deal more effectively with the young.

On the question of who should take responsibility for rehabilitative effort, a majority of the educational leaders, 63 per cent, said that they and others in the community have equal responsibility.

Three-quarters of the economic and religious leaders said it was primarily a job for someone else, mostly parents.

Therapeutic and corrective agencies saw a major role for themselves, and did not see the school as highly relevant for rehabilitative work.

In a reciprocal way, the school leaders did not see the law enforcement and therapeutic agencies as significantly important influences for change in youth development.

Without pursuing the data further at this point, I shall summarize what seem to be several highlights of the functioning of the professional socialization community:

First, there is a widespread agreement in attributing to parents most of the blame for deviancy and delinquency among youth. But there is little mention of goals or significant programs involving parents or collaboration with parents to strengthen family leadership. There are significant differences in ideas about what should be done and by whom, and a significant lack of coordination, in terms of frequency and subject of conversation, between the leaders across segments.

I would now like to go to a second level of functioning

of the socialization community. We have talked about the top influentials; they are the policy and program leaders. The day-to-day interaction process of socializing the young is, of course, carried on by a large network of direct workers: teachers, counselors, "big brothers," club leaders, scoutmasters, recreational leaders, and so on. What kind of team work is there at this level?

The answer is that there is far less communication here than among the program leaders. We secured the names of some two hundred direct workers whom program leaders viewed as the most creative and visible group and individual workers with the young in all segments of the community. When a sample of them were invited to meet, we found them quite ignorant of each other's practices or of each other's clients. There was no process of exchange of information across programs.

In a more intensive study of some ten elementary and secondary schools, we found that colleagues in the same building do not share their classroom innovations with other classrooms.

Again summarizing our findings: at the level of direct work with the young there is a lack of communication or coordination among the socialization agents, a general exclusion of parents, and lack of connection with family life. Those viewed as being both most influential and also most amateur are the most neglected and isolated members of the child- and youth-development team.

Before leaving this diagnosis of the socialization community, let me point to another problem which I think is just as serious as that of communication and coordination. This is the problem of personnel recruitment and training.

As the National Commission on National Health has pointed out, the most serious social and educational need in every community is that of effective recruiting and training of volunteer and subprofessional manpower. To be effective this must be a cooperative task for the various socialization agencies, and continuous and high priority must be given to high-quality programs of in-service training. These programs can be sustained only by cooperative interagency training programs.

I have recently had a number of conversations about these data with school board members who are from industry. They usually express surprise and dismay at the lack of well-developed in-service–education programs with highly qualified training officers in school systems and in other child- and youth-development agencies of the community. As one of them put it, "How is it that we can keep our agricultural practitioners, the farmers, linked so closely to new research and practice, but have so little going on to link educational practitioners with new research and new developments in raising children? We seem to value our efficiency in raising hogs and creating new machines more than our efficiency in raising kids." We'll return to this problem later when we look at some of the concrete potentialities for improving youth-development practice.

It is time now to turn from the community to the children and youth whom we are trying to help and who seem so often to deviate from our plans for their education and maturation.

The Youth Culture

Viewing the young as a peer society with a variety of subcultures and collective standards, teachers and other youth workers are tempted and have a tendency to view the classroom or club situation as ones in which they as adult leaders have the major influence over the learning or behavior of each child in the group. They see the situation as one of a relationship between themselves and each of the learners, pupils, students, group members.

But research analyses reveal instead a complex social structure of peers in which motivation to learn and patterns of relationship towards adults are highly determined by group standards and the interpersonal evaluations among the children. Sociometric studies of junior and senior high groups have shown that the antischool and the proschool students tend to form separate societies, with a good deal of mutual antagonism and avoidance. Race and social class also influence the formation of substructures in the school. A number of studies show that the students' positions in the peer group remain quite stable from fall to spring and from year to year; for example, from October to June the correlations in status position within the classroom range from 70 to 95.

What difference do these findings make to educational objectives? Some of the major findings from both elementary- and secondary-classroom studies indicate that classmates who are disliked, when matched for IQ, with classmates who are liked, do not fully use their intellectual capacity. Being disliked is especially dysfunctional for girls. Classmates evaluated as low in influence status also fail to use fully their innate ability; low-influence status is especially dysfunctional for boys. The rejected low-status peers evaluate themselves, their school work, and the teacher more negatively than do their higher-status peers of equal intellectual ability.

In the same school and classroom climates, often one path to status is open to the low-status child: he can demonstrate boldness in resisting and testing adult authority. If there is a general feeling in the group that the adult leadership is noxious in some way, then peer status can be achieved in this way.

Let's turn now to a different aspect of the classroom or group situation, the cross-generational relations between the adults and the young. In one study of all elementary classrooms in one school, we made a series of quantitative classroom observations of teacher-pupil interaction. This was in a highly rated school with a well-trained professional staff. One of the major findings was that the children who had low status among their peers were also most frequently criticized and least frequently rewarded by their teacher. Aggressive, low-achievement boys particularly were rejected. The teachers were not aware of this pattern. In short, the teachers were in unconscious collusion with the peers in providing a failure and exclusion experience for these particular children.

Wormell's [1] study of under-achievement in junior high school indicates that communication and support from parents is much less active and positive for under-achievers than for high-achievers of the same intellectual ability. Schmuck [2] and Van Egmond [3] have confirmed this finding in larger studies of populations of elementary and secondary classrooms.

The low-achieving student's rejection of adults and adult efforts to help are supported usually by a small group of like-minded peers; and the teacher's efforts to exert more control on these pupils are supported both by her own impulses and by the expectations of her colleagues.

I would now like to view the classroom in a third way, as a cross-age peer culture.

Most children grow up in a cross-age peer culture of brothers and sisters and neighborhood associates. By observing older children, young ones learn how to behave

toward and cope with grownups. They also experience the
patterns of teasing, exploitation, and ignoring behavior from
the older ones. Their desires to respect and to emulate are
mixed with needs to defend themselves and even to retaliate.
The influence of older children as antisocial models is well
known in the work on delinquency. The use of older peers
as educational helpers and socializers was a customary pattern in the rural school. Very little systematic research has
been undertaken on the role of cross-age relationships in the
school system. We are just beginning some experimentation,
to which I'll refer in a moment. But let me express a belief
at this point that cross-age peer relations are one of the very
potent forces in the school system at all age levels—forces
either toward rejection of learning or toward the acceptance
of learning.

A study of pupil perceptions of the values and expectations of their classmates has revealed one very important
restraint on active cooperation in learning activities between
the teacher and the young. Frequently a majority of the
students in a classroom perceive that a majority of their
peers are against too much commitment to school work, too
much recitation, too much cooperation with the teacher;
while on private questionnaires a majority in the class says
that personally they would like to be more active in learning
and have more relationship with the teacher. This inhibiting
state of pluralistic ignorance, as it is called by the sociologist,
continues as long as there is no occasion to share and discuss their personal values.

An even more disturbing barrier to creative cross-
generation relations in the classroom has been revealed in
some interviews with teachers who have entered new teaching assignments with enthusiastic plans for sharing the planning and execution of the educational adventure with their

students, but very soon have felt the disapproval of their older, higher-status colleagues that such nonsense may give the students wrong ideas.

Students confirm that very often a new teacher is "swell" for a couple of years until she gets "spoiled." "Fear of what my colleagues would think" frequently comes up as a strong restraining force and it seems to inhibit more active efforts at educational collaboration with the students.

To summarize then, first I believe one can say that negative, alienative relations between many students and teachers develop and continue because from past experience both students and teachers are oriented toward a relationship of mutual distrust. Second, a history of failure at academic tasks often prejudices many students against another probable failure experience, so that the well-motivated and often well-designed efforts of good teachers are rejected. Finally, I would like to view the school as a system of organized teamwork among professional educators.

The School System

I shan't try to summarize the diagnostic research on the school system as an organization—Albert Reiss, Neal Gross, and other students of school organization are better equipped than I—but from our research activities I would like to offer three interpretations.

First, as I see it, most students' relationship to the school system is quite parallel to that of many first-line employees to business and government organizations: the participation and involvement in planning and decision making stops at the level just above them. As a result of the research and analyses of Argyris, MacGregor, Hare, Likert, Kahn, Mann, and others, the situation is changing rapidly in business organizations. Many managers now see the most productive pattern of relationships as one of "participative management," in which overlapping committees, task groups, or working groups link all levels of the organization in diagnosis of problems, in the projecting of plans, and in commitments to action. Students, on the other hand, do not have this type of involvement in the design and execution of their learning experiences.

Second, there is a remarkable lack of communication among teachers about their classroom practices, their educational goals, and their efforts to help particular students.

Third, teachers tend to perceive their administrators as reacting negatively to innovations in curriculum organization, teaching practices, and the more active involvement of students in evaluating and influencing the educational system.

Summary of Diagnostic Observations

I shall try to summarize the diagnostic observations in such a way as to provide a link with some examples of directions of effort.

At the community level, first, there seems to be a lack of communication and coordination among youth-development leaders and also among direct workers, and a lack of joint effort in locating recruiting, and training the needed manpower. There is a variety of significant unresolved differences among the leaders as to what should be done and by whom.

Second, parents are most often cited as a major cause of misbehavior, but there is relatively little significant effort at the involvement and in-service training of parents.

Third, at the level of school system, there is a lack of effort to involve young learners in the goals and functions of the educational process. Second, the efficiency values of the educational administrators (our experiences were primarily with principals and single schools) conflict with our knowledge of effective education, particularly of the effective education of deviant and alienated learners.

Fourth, there is a lack of shared commitment and communication among colleagues in developing and improving educational practices.

Finally, pupils are permitted to have educational experiences that produce and nurture increasingly serious alienation from the teacher, the school, and the learning tasks, so that they may become a separated subpopulation within the peer culture.

At the youth culture level, first there is typically a peer interpersonal evaluation process that frequently creates an unhealthy mental health situation and a poorly motivated learning situation for a significant number of students. I'm referring to middle-class suburban classrooms as well as to lower-class metropolitan classrooms. Sometimes segregated subcultures develop along lines of social class or race. In other cases the separation is between a prosocial, prolearning population and one whose behavior is antisocial. Peer-group evaluations divide the child and youth culture on other levels as well.

Second, the status process in the peer group provokes and encourages some students to find attention and recognition through antiteacher and antilearning behavior.

Finally, there is a potent cross-age peer influence which is neglected as an educational force.

§   Designs for Action: Examples

Now we shall look at some brief illustrations of action designs related to these diagnostic points. In collaboration with educators and other youth workers, our team of social scientists has used data from the type of studies summarized here to derive action designs and to formulate alternative approaches to cope with particular problems.

This social engineering task should utilize our scientific knowledge to formulate some effective revisions of educational practice. Let me give you some "snap shots" of what has emerged. I want to make one footnote however: all our young social scientist-engineers were rewarded to find in almost every school building teachers who had developed creative practices in line with some of these derivations, but who were unaware of the significance of their inventions, were not able to verbalize them, and certainly were unable or not motivated to communicate them.

As a result, we have a great wealth of innovative practices which are being lost by lack of description, documentation, evaluation, articulation and diffusion to peers. However, many new images of practice are emerging as scientists and practitioners use the opportunity to collaborate.

Working with the Socialization Community

First, at the community level, a seminar was held for selected-program leaders from each of the six areas mentioned earlier. Thirty leaders were selected as being key figures in the six areas, and twenty-seven responded positively by coming and staying with it.

The seminar started with a feed-back phase, looking at the research data, and then moved into discussion and planning. The early feed-back sessions presented a series of dramatic episodes of interaction selected to represent the data. The community leaders were able to view these episodes and then think about them in terms of their own experiences. The researcher could say to what degree a particular behavioral episode was typical of the relationship, for example, between delinquent boys and their fathers. The seminar then sought to define issues by active discussion between the judge, the school administrator, Council of Social Agencies administrator, and so forth. This process became very significant as the participants began to listen to each other.

The third phase was that of setting up problem work groups, or task forces, which worked with consultation from one member of the university team. Four work groups developed out of the seminar: one on designs for rehabilitation of delinquents, one on delinquency prevention, a third on values education, and one on coordination of services in relation to the family.

A second community-level experiment was the nomination and then invitation of about thirty-five direct workers across the community agencies to join a community youth leaders' seminar. This again started with a feed-back process, grew into a concern with criteria for good practice, and then developed into a process for exchanging innovations. The members are now preparing a booklet describing their innovations and practices, which can be used across all agencies, including the school. Most of the consulting help was on how to conceptualize, how to articulate, and how to describe effective practice.

A third activity was the development at the state level of the Michigan Laboratory for Workers with Youth. This involved about twenty of the youth-serving agencies of the state, including the Department of Public Instruction and the Michigan Education Association, sponsored by Michigan State University, Wayne State University, and the University of Michigan. There have been three laboratories, in which the exciting thing to me was that the educators reported that one of the most significant learning experiences for them was the dialogue with professional agency leaders outside the school system.

A fourth activity, in some ways the most difficult, was the job of identifying the trainers of youth workers in the community. Who trains the volunteers, subprofessionals, and inservice trainers of teachers, boy scout leaders, mental health workers, parents, and so on? We are now examining the possibility of future programs of in-service training which cut across all community socialization agencies.

Working with the School System

Moving down to the level of the school system, let me mention several efforts derived from our diagnostic work. Teachers in several school systems responded actively when given the opportunity to engage in diagnostic research about what was going on in their classrooms that effected motivation to learn and good mental health.

At faculty meetings there was a brief presentation of the opportunity to collaborate and each teacher was given a chance to leave a slip indicating his interest in talking further about this opportunity. We had so many volunteers that it was difficult to select a group small enough to handle effectively. This was at elementary and at junior and senior high levels.

The cooperating teachers began by collecting data in their classrooms. Some instruments required that the teachers formulate their own approach to teaching and their own philosophy of education. A workshop period followed in which the teachers were helped to interpret their data and, in collaboration with a consultant, to plan changes in practice that seemed to be indicated by analyses of the data about themselves and their classrooms.

One interesting innovation developed when the teachers faced the problem of doing something differently in their own classrooms which they felt was potentially dangerous; there were all kinds of images of awkwardness and difficulty. So a squad of children was recruited to come in and help, giving the teachers a chance to practice new approaches. This team of eleven- and twelve-year-old pupils developed a great enthusiasm for their role as teacher trainers. When the teachers wanted to try out, some kind of technique before "playing for keeps," and to get feedback, the pupils were available.

Another interesting development occurred when one or two teachers felt a strong need for support at the time they were beginning a new approach but felt that they couldn't find that support within their own building. So they developed a cross-building clinic at which they met every three weeks all winter. Although some of them drove sixty or seventy miles, they never missed this chance to share problems, to talk freely about failure, and to seek help from each other. This failure to find support for innovations from other teachers in their building was one of the most significant eye-openers regarding the problems of in-service training within the building.

Another action design grew out of the interest in spreading significant new practices. The idea developed of forming "diffusion teams" to see to what extent some thirty or forty new practices developed by these teachers could be spread to others. The teachers helped to write a brochure called "Inventory of Teaching Innovations Directed toward Improving Classroom Learning Atmospheres." Three-person "diffusion teams" (the principal, a collaborating teacher, and an outside consultant) were formed for each building to see if these innovations could be linked from the experimentation to the interests of the other teachers in the buildings.

One of the interesting outcomes was that the teachers by and large regarded the use of someone else's practice as "imitation" and therefore to be looked down on. For perspective, we looked at the search for innovation in the areas of medicine, industry, and agriculture, and observed the great value these disciplines placed on adoption and creative adaptation. By and large this was a tremendously eye-opening experience for the teachers who had regarded the notion of imitating somebody else in the building as "low status."

Another activity design that developed was cross-generational training, that is, direct training of adults and young together. We tried this three times with family units, and are planning to try some teacher-pupil units. The interesting discovery about family units was the need for a phase when the mothers, the fathers, and the teenagers could meet separately to talk about their problems of communication. Then there came a phase when they could look at family-life episodes (produced by role-playing) while they sat in family-like units, units in which no one sat with a member of his own family. A mother, father, a daughter or a son sat in a diagnostic family team, but none was from the same family. They observed typical family crises that had been mentioned in previous discussion. After a number of sessions of this kind they began to sit in family units and openly discuss these family events similar to their own. Then they were ready to discuss their own relations in family sessions. We believe this type of design will be an effective approach to teacher-student relations.

Working with the Youth Culture

Let me now give two or three examples of experimentation at the peer-system level. The first experiment focused on the involvement of the student group in the goals and evaluation of learning.

In a fifth grade, biracial and mixed social class, the teacher's diagnosis described three of the five top-status members of the class as among the most antilearning, antiteacher members of the class.

From her sociometric data, the teacher appointed a classroom steering committee which included two antisocial leaders and two prosocial leaders. She convened them for a bag lunch, which she provided the first time, and presented the notion, "Wouldn't it be worthwhile to find out what the whole class thought were signs of having a good day, or a bad day, in the classroom?" She worked with them on leading this discussion.

They presented to the class the question, "If a visitor from Russia came into their class and knew nothing about American classrooms, what would be signs that we were having a bad day of learning things and feeling unhappy in our classroom, and what would be signs that we were having a good day?" They made two lists on the board and each day one member of the steering committee served as an evaluation and research person: he kept a list of events, and during the last half hour he reviewed what he thought were the signs of a good day or a bad day. He voiced whatever recommendations came to his mind about what could be done tomorrow to improve their day.

At the end of the week, the steering committee had the last hour to discuss the whole week and to lead discussion on reactions to their observations and recommendations. At the end of the two weeks, they appointed the next steering committee, which in turn appointed the next one, and so on.

Some interesting evidence of movement in the social structure came in the fifth week when the boy who had been second in power, and the most antisocial, came to the teacher and said he felt that the kids weren't listening and paying so much attention to him; what should he do? He had gone down in fact to the twelfth position in socio-metric structure, and was interested finally in getting help. Thus began the process of effective student-teacher relationship for several pupils.

Another interesting process began when some of the teachers found the courage to get data from the pupils as to how they felt about various aspects of the teaching. The most effective process was one in which the children rated the teacher on a number of scales and drew lines to where they wished she were. At the same time the teacher rated the classroom on a series of dimensions as she saw it, and then as she wished it to be. These ratings were displayed and used in the reciprocal analysis of their wishes for each other.

Another very exciting adventure was one in which, at a community level, nominations were secured of teenage leaders: Negro, white, lower-class, middle-class, antisocial, prosocial. They were invited to a community teen-leadership seminar. They began by looking at data from studies of the causes of problems between adults and young people in the community. They then proceeded to examine the kinds of unhealthy divisions within their peer society. The tapes of these meetings contain, for example, a monologue of a middle-class boy talking about the feelings he has when walking down the high-school corridor with a Negro friend, seeing another friend coming, wondering how he will react, and wishing he didn't feel that way, but he does. Presentations of this sort led the teen-agers to have a week-end retreat to discuss relations among teen-agers, out of which came two comittees: a committee to train parents and teachers, and a committee to write a pamphlet on teen-age feelings about relations with adults. They had a series of sessions on an invitation basis with parents and teachers; the adults' response to this invitation was very encouraging.

Just one example from the area of cross-age peer relations: In a lower-class, biracial school, and also in a middle-class laboratory school, we decided to test the notion that perhaps some of the most helpful influences on motivation to learn and on actual skill-learning in the first three grades might come from sixth-graders. We had some data on how these ages perceived each other, and we recognized that there were some problems, for example, of punitive and teasing orientations of olders toward youngers. Before the eager volunteers from the sixth grade were permitted to begin their work, they attended a bi-weekly, half-hour seminar on "olders helping youngers." The seminar continued throughout their field work, so that the older children could bring up problems and issues related to their assignments. They did a great deal of role-playing of their problems of tutoring.

Let me give you a brief example of cross-age help. An aggressive boy in kindergarten was having a temper tantrum and knocked down some material other children were using. He was sent to the corner, and when the teacher went over and asked if she could do anything to help him think about this, he said, "Please send for Jim." Jim was the most acting-out boy in the team of sixth-grade helpers. He came down from his room for a few minutes, and after the situation was explained to him, he went over and talked to the boy for a few minutes. The boy got up and rejoined his classmates (he had been told that when he felt he could join the group again, it was OK), and began playing quietly. As Jim was leaving the teacher asked how he had helped. He said, "Well, I just told him, that this is the way I used to behave all the time, and I still do too much, and you sure miss out on a lot of fun that way, and the other kids won't like you."

Of course the teacher could have said the same thing, but it wouldn't have had the same kind of effect.

The exuberance of these youngsters in developing this kind of helping skill and sensitivity is coupled with reports from the sixth-grade teacher that the helpers showed quite an upward spurt in their own academic motivation as a result of their responsibilities.

Many creative practitioners, of course, have come up with inventions similar to and superior to these. The major point, I think, is that one can collect, in collaboration with practitioners, scientific data that will provide a sound basis for innovations and their evaluation. And if the collaboration emphasizes documentation, then diffusion to others can occur.

Summary of Observations about Research Utilization

In conclusion, it seems to me that much waste could be eliminated in educational experimentation, in new-product development as the industrialists think of it, if diagnostic research or action research were recognized as a most efficient way of achieving the innovation and diffusion of effective educational practices.

Second, the diffusion of new creative practices is much

more difficult than the invention. This is the area of greatest waste at the moment in such fields as delinquency prevention and work with the dropout, the retarded, etc.

The research knowledge and the conceptual perspective needed to design sound programs will usually not be found in the staff of operating agencies. Outsiders, often university-based collaborators, are one of the best sources of efficient and active product development. The same holds true, I think, for locating the best manpower resources for in-service training of the staff. In several fields the techniques of in-service training have developed far beyond current training practice in education. We must use these resources just as fully as we use scientific resources.

Finally, by taking the initiative in stimulating the cooperation of other agencies and in demonstrating innovative programs, I think the school has the most central opportunity to exert leadership in the community.

Notes

1. Helen E. Wormell, "A Comparative Study of Perceptions Related to Self, Home, and School among Selected Ninth-grade Students" (unpublished doctoral dissertation, University of Michigan, 1963).

2. Richard A. Schmuck, "Some Relationships of Peer-Liking Patterns in the Classroom to Pupil Attitudes and Achievement," *The School Review*, Vol. LXXI, No. 3 (University of Chicago Press, Autumn, 1963).

3. Elmer E. Van Egmond, "Social Interrelationship Skills and Effective Utilization of Intelligence in the Classroom" (unpublished doctoral dissertation, University of Michigan, 1960).

READING: LARGE ISSUES, SPECIFIC PROBLEMS, AND POSSIBLE SOLUTIONS

S. Alan Cohen

§ Introduction

The "expanding role of the school" is a cliché that ante-dates our current social issues: John Dewey spent a lifetime propagating this theme; Horace Mann recognized it almost a century before Dewey; and Jefferson spoke of education's vital role in the new democracy as early as 1779. Professional educators have encouraged social leaders to recognize the school's role as an agent of social control or change, but much of what they have said has fallen on ears not ready to listen.

Now, social crisis has brought federal and foundation money to the doors of urban schools. Automation, unemployment, segregation, delinquency, cultural conflict, over-population, and a general depersonalization of man have stimulated the keepers of the research purse to action. With the challenge of the crisis and the hope of research dollars have also come the social scientists; they come to tell the educator about the school's expanding role and to convince

30656

him of his need for help from allied professions. Amazed by this attention and unprepared for large-scale research and development, the educator alternates between defending his practices and expressing enthusiasm for new responsibilities.

There has been little time to build efficient lines of communication between these "peripheral" professions and the school, but because the social crisis cannot wait the social sciences have joined forces to turn the school into the agent of social control and change that educators have long envisioned. *What kind of administrative decisions will be made under this new alliance, and what effects will they have on youth and community?*

One potential weakness of this new alliance is that both sides lose sight of the school's core function. This paper will attempt to define this core function, describe its relationship to social crisis, and cite three specific problems that must be solved to fulfill this function. The last section of this paper will describe a methodological model for classroom teaching, some educational guidelines to action, and some effects of the model upon youth. I have used the teaching of reading to illustrate my theme because it is the area that currently receives most of my attention.

This paper does not advocate restricting the school's role in society; instead, it offers both the educational administrator and his new allies a guideline for making decisions involving the school. My hypothesis is that by fulfilling its core function the school can make its greatest contribution to youth and the community.

§   Large Issues

If education is a profession, what is its unique job?
Some leading educators have been thinking aloud on this
question lately. Perhaps it is impertinent for me to echo
or add to what Durrell (19) or Gates has said, but it is
germane to my message about the teaching of reading.
Furthermore, the question is particularly relevant to issues
currently facing educators, such issues as integration, religion, sex education, juvenile delinquency, auto insurance
rates, and driver training. One wonders where, if anywhere,
the school's domain ends and other professional worlds
begin. For example, I often find it difficult to distinguish
my own role from that of psychologist, psychiatrist, neurolo-
gist, social worker, family physician, clergyman, and politi-
cian. Classroom teachers and school administrators could
add accountant, lawyer, and policeman to that list.

Certainly, effective educators must play many roles.
The demands of any profession require functions that reach
across professional boundaries: the lawyer plays marriage
counselor, while the policeman occasionally plays midwife
or administers to the psychosocial needs of juvenile delinquents. But every profession has a boundary line that
demarcates certain functions as unique to that profession:
these are a profession's core or primary functions that must
receive top priority. The ability and legal authority to perform these functions makes one a member of a particular
profession.

When I successfully cross professional boundaries to
borrow activities that enhance my own core functions, I
increase my effectiveness as a professional educator. The
ability to perform activities relevant to my other roles as

community leader, citizen, or father adds to my stature as a professional, but it never relieves me of the obligation to perform the core functions of my own profession.

Some educators have lost sight of their core function, that the educator's job is, in Dr. Donald Durrell's words (19), "to increase the quantity and quality of learning." As a result, professional education in general, and teaching of reading in particular, has suffered.

No other profession can claim as its core function the development and application of theories and techniques to increase the amount and quality of learning. Whatever else I do, I cannot call myself a professional educator unless I am basically concerned with operations that increase learning efficiency. Furthermore, by neglecting my core function, I am not fulfilling my social obligation to youth and community.

Why have some professional educators neglected this unique obligation? In his quest for methods to increase the quantity and quality of education, John Dewey urged educators to cross professional boundaries for knowledge and techniques. Dewey also recognized the role of the school as a social force. (11) He emphasized that professional educators must recognize their potential as agents of social change. But at no time did Dewey lose sight of the core functions of education.

Unfortunately, some of his successors have not shared his perspicacity. Reconstructionism in American philosophy of education advocates, for example, that the principal job of the school is to initiate or promote social change. (9:319-24) Theodore Brameld, reconstructionisms's leading voice, defines the direction of change and advocates education for world government as the educator's primary concern. (8)

Thus, those educators who have not accepted the up-

grading of learning as their primary obligation have not fulfilled their unique function. Yet as citizens, social leaders,
and professional educators we might agree with Brameld's
desire to promote world government, and we might even
act upon that desire. In so doing, however, we would not
only thereby be sharing a function with other social leaders,
other professionals, and with other responsible citizens of
any vocation or profession; but we would also *not* be fulfilling our unique service to the community as professional
educators.

Consider an analogous situation. The personal counseling offered by my family physiican adds to his professional
competence. I admire his active support of social reform
and his concern for education, but he is first and foremost
a diagnostician and healer. Never could all his other attributes substitute for basic professional competence.

As educators we want to help resolve the social problems of our day: we would act decisively one way or another
on the church-state issue, and perhaps on juvenile delinquency, too, which is also a major concern of the school.
But our first job as professional educators is to upgrade
learning. Therefore, we should not commit ourselves to
careers in professional education unless we are willing to
dedicate ourselves to increasing the quantity and quality
of learning. In fact, even when we do other things which
may add to our professional competency, they cannot
substitute for our core function.

In serving this function, we may discover that our
greatest contribution to social change *is* through upgrading
learning in the classroom. For example, can we say we
know how to teach culturally deprived youngsters to read,
that we can do this efficiently and with certainty if we get
enough money and specific types of materials and facilities?

When we can say this with certainty, we will offer the community a greater service in remedying social inequities. We must start now to solve the learning problems of disadvantaged children. We cannot do this with vigor until professional educators recognize their core function and spend less time and energy politicking with pressure groups or juggling school enrollments according to race and color, and more on educational technology. In every community, educators must unite and demonstrate to the public that they will no longer allow the school to be blamed for every social disease or national crisis from Sputnik to juvenile delinquency, from low morals to high traffic death rates. At the same time, we must be prepared to plunge vigorously into our professional function of upgrading learning in our schools.

If the first reason for not fulfilling our professional function is the failure to accept that function; the second reason is a result of the first. We know how little we know about learning. In defense of our deficiencies we assume many functions thrust upon us by the family, by other professions, and by sectors of the community: we have become responsible for instilling a fear of God, for controlling the labor market, for teaching about sex, for reducing highway death rates, for preventing (or causing) juvenile delinquency, for solving (or contributing to) the social problems of disadvantaged children, for closing the missile gap between Russia and the West, for preventing (or causing) mental illness. Perhaps we assume these extra responsibilities to hide our inadequacies and to appease our sense of guilt.

A few months ago one of Mobilization for Youth's street workers, a skilled social worker, came to me for some advice about four delinquent eighth-graders with whom he had been working. He had discovered they lacked the basic skills of reading and writing. In less than a month he had taught these youngsters to read simple fourth-grade material. He had come to me for suggestions about material and techniques.

"Do you know," he exclaimed, "they didn't know the alphabet or the sounds of some letter combinations!" His bewilderment was a comment on the failure of my profession to fulfill core function. What had the school been doing for eight years? How could four boys sit in school day after day (less truancies), ten months per year, for eight years without mastering the alphabet? What had a street worker done incidental to his core function that the professional educator could not do?

Have the schools so burdened themselves with varied jobs, that they have neglected to perfect their basic responsibility, which is to teach every youngster to read and write? In Puerto Rican New York or in Chicago's Black Belt the fact that cultural conflict, language barriers, and a host of other factors complicate the process is no excuse for failing to do our job. It is, in fact, added reason to cast aside peripheral tasks and plunge into the core functions of education —to upgrade the learning *at least* of reading and writing.

Teacher-training institutions reflect a similar dilemma. In four years they must provide every prospective teacher with a liberal arts education, and they must prepare him for all the responsibilities of the profession. How much time is left for colleges to teach the technology of teaching reading? Mary Austin's study is a partial answer to this question. (3)

In the end, the superintendent of schools or the principal must hire a reading consultant. If we try to hold the principal responsible for professional know-how, he replies,

"But I'm not a reading specialist," or "I'm no psychologist." What functions can we expect an administrator or teacher to perform that a member of no other profession can perform?

These same teachers and administrators must deal with local lay educators who think they know the best methods of teaching reading. If educators know little about learning to read, they must expect difficulty from people like Mr. Trace, who knows something about how Ivan learns to read but less about how Johnny reads. (22) But some educators' lack of professional know-how has offered pseudo experts fertile grounds on which to proliferate. How many professional educators know more about the teaching of reading than Professors Trace or Walcutt? (23) More important, how much of the educator's time is spent finding out more about the teaching and learning of reading?

SUMMARY OF LARGE ISSUES

Some educators have failed to define their unique professional role; others have defined it, but have failed to assume that role. For various reasons educators become involved in peripheral issues. Such issues are certainly within the professional educator's domain, but they are not central to his profession. The core function of educational administration and classroom teaching is to increase the quantity and quality of learning. Until he gives this function his top priority, the educator will be plagued, on one hand, by added social responsibilities that are more appropriately obligations of other sectors of the society and, on the other hand, by pseudo educators who insist they know more about educational technology than do the professionals.

The greatest service a professional educator can offer

to his community is the ability to teach its children to read, write, do arithmetic, and learn a variety of skills and attitudes that society and students feel are important to have. Before he says, "I can help desegregate the community," or "I can reduce the juvenile crime rate in this city," the professional educator must first say, "I can teach reading (for example) with certainty." For this is the domain through which we educators can, in fact, help solve some of the social problems of our day.

§   Specific Problems

The latest word about Mark Hopkins on one end of a log is that he was no educational bargain. (10) Nevertheless, the principle of that aphorism remains valid if we replace President Hopkins with Mr. Chips, or Sylvia Ashton-Warner, or even a half-competent pedagogue. Why is a one-to-one teacher-student ratio so potentially effective?

First, the learning can be adapted to the individual. The learning program need not fit the mode, median, or mean of any group, heterogeneous or homogeneous. What the pupil already knows is respected, so that learning can involve new skills, content, attitudes, and perceptions. Thus, the *content of learning* fits the individual's needs.

Second, the *level of content* can be tailored to the single student's level of capacity and achievement. A personal tutor can translate information about ninth-grade algebra into fourth-grade vocabulary for the "low verbal, high math" pupil.

Third, the *speed of teaching* can be adjusted to the pupil's learning pace. He need not waste one day on three pages of word drills waiting for fifteen classmates to master the concept of comparative degree in English modifiers. Nor must he plunge into the superlative degree of adjectives if he has not yet grasped the positive degree. He moves at his own pace.

Finally, the *frequency of response* to teaching stimuli is intensified in the one-to-one relationship. The tutored student is always on the spot. He always works, always acts, and never has to wait his turn. He is always next. This is active learning *par excellence*.

Certainly, much is to be gained in a group. There are potentials for social-personal experiences, enrichment, motivation, variety, and sheer fun that the one-to-one teacher-learner system cannot provide. But some crucial variables not easily supplied in the group have long been selling points of tutorial education. One-to-one teaching-learning is highly efficient because it can provide for individual content needs, levels, speed, and frequencies of learning.

The first specific problem in increasing the quantity and quality of learning in mass education is the difficulty of providing for individualized needs of content, level, speed, and frequency of action.

Homogeneous grouping is no solution. Research shows generally no significant differences in school achievement due to homogeneous grouping. (12) The reason may be that grouping per se does not individualize level, speed, or frequency of action; nor does it provide for specific content needs of individuals; nor does it automatically increase motivation. I suspect that the academic successes of a Boston Latin School or Bronx High School of Science alumnus are due less to his superior education and more to his superior capacity. Abramson's study on this population supports my hunch. (1) I am less impressed with Andover and Exeter academies than I am with their students. These are the same types of students whose scholarship impressed me during my first year of teaching—in an understaffed, poorly financed, third-rate rural high school. They learned in spite of the quality of education. For the rest of the population, however, grouping by itself does not increase the quantity and quality of learning unless individualized content, level, speed, and frequency of active learning are achieved. With a thirty-to-one student-teacher ratio, something in addition to grouping is needed to upgrade learning.

For example, common practice still groups students according to intelligence. Yet, any competent psychologist can advise the educator that two 110 IQ's on a Wechsler-Bellevue Intelligence Scale for Children are alike only by arithmetic accident. One score probably represents an entirely different subtest scatter than the other. One's liabilities may be the other's assets. Two youngsters represented by these numbers are as qualitatively different as any two people can be.

The same is true of reading achievement scores. Our research shows that in a group of students testing at fifth-grade level in reading, the spread of scores for any specific reading subskill is normally distributed. (4) Furthermore, the spread of most reading subskill scores for the top quartile of readers is not very different from that of the bottom quartile of readers. (5) This means, for example, that on the Iowa Silent Reading Test, five tenth-graders can earn a total reading grade level of 11.0 *for five different reasons.* Johnnie may be a whiz at locating information; Tom may be strong in vocabulary and sentence meaning; Bill may excel on speed of comprehension, and so on. Tom may be below average on the specific subskill on which Bill excels; yet both earn reading grade levels of 11.0. Do both have the same reading needs? Can the needs of each be solved by grouping according to their common reading grade level?

How many schools group students "homogeneously" according to reading grade levels and then assume that they all read approximately the same? Phil reads at grade level 9.5; his paragraph comprehension is two grade levels above Tom's score. Yet, Tom's reading grade level is 11.0. The need to adjust instruction to individual needs in content, level, speed, and frequency of activity is just as great in so-called "homogeneous" groups as in so-called "heterogeneous" groups. Grouping a class into "high" readers or "low" readers, Spanish-speaking Puerto Ricans or English-speaking Puerto Ricans, Mississippi or Detroit Negroes does not solve the problem of individualizing instruction.

The second specific problem in upgrading learning is to affect "quality of learning," and consists first of defining *quality* operationally. If Phil increases his reading achievement by two grade levels in one year of school, have we increased quality or quantity? Have we affected understanding, appreciation, or creativity? Can Phil think critically, in depth, elaboratively? What effect has learning had on Phil's psychosocial behavior? Have basic perceptions of himself and the world around him changed?

Teachers have talked of these qualities for decades, but we still do not have reliable or valid measurements of them. How can we know we increase quality if we cannot measure it? We are just beginning to scratch the surface of this problem. Under the labels of research in creativity, problem solving, and cognitive styles some breakthroughs seem imminent.

Again, I wonder how many public school administrators set aside time each week with their professional staffs to tackle this problem of quality of learning. Let them try to define it operationally, try to observe it, and then try to teach for it.

There are some obvious places to begin this search for quality. For example, what does our reading research imply when it shows that a student's achievement on a multiple-choice test is significantly different from his achievement on a written-recall test? Does this reflect a qualitative difference in behavior? Research shows that college graduates with adequate reading achievement scores read only one book per year on the average. Is this a problem of educational quality?

This year, in particular, I have grave doubts about the quality of instruction in the "larger" goals of the curriculum. In a nation whose social problems include automation, unemployment, juvenile delinquency, and discrimination, we still find so-called educated persons opposed to social reform for culturally deprived people. Just how effective is education toward wider goals in Boston, for example?

As in most large cities, Boston's civil rights battle has been fought in the schools. Unfortunate as this is, in the last Boston school-committee election, the "silk stocking" precincts joined the rest of the citizenry in defeating the reform candidates. A group of anti-desegregation candidates received the largest plurality in the history of Boston school-committee elections. But at election time less money was being spent to educate Negro children than white children in Boston schools; the facilities in Negro schools were shockingly inadequate; and *de facto* segregation did exist, even though it was not the school's fault.

Most of the "silk stocking" voters were at least high school graduates. They are products of our schools. Is all the talk about more social studies, education for democracy, and moral ideals in the schools just so much hog wash? Has education failed to increase quality of learning of these values? Do the products of American schools emerge with a sense of social responsibility? In the face of such election results, can we say that we have increased the quantity and quality of learning social studies?

The emphasis here is on effectiveness of instruction regardless of content. Obviously, the church and the home have not taught these values adequately. History bears testimony to this inadequacy. If the modern school assumes major responsibility for teaching these attitudes (and I am not sure it should), then it must seriously consider the technology of increasing the quality of learning. Otherwise, it should hand back to other sectors of the community the major responsibility for teaching the "larger" values.

Personally, I have enough difficulty teaching reading, the larger part of which involves attitudes. Realizing the problems of increasing quality of learning in this specific area, I am not very optimistic about the probability of the school's success in teaching the "larger values," at least not at this stage of learning technology.

A third specific problem in education, and especially in reading, is the wide gulf between the results of educational research and classroom practices. In addition to lack of *knowledge* about educational research, some administrators and teachers lack a positive *attitude* toward research.

Not long ago, I persuaded a master reading teacher to match her talents against a teaching machine in a controlled experiment. Her department head tried to prevent the experiment by arguing: "I don't believe in teaching machines." Fortunately, the principal intervened, and the experiment took place. The machine taught Latin and Greek affixes and structural analysis of words more efficiently than the master teacher. Both the students and the teacher were delighted with the machine, but the department head was unswayed: "I still don't believe in teaching machines." The principal shrugged his shoulders and murmured something about "retirement in two years, so why fight it."

The irony of this attitude toward research within the profession is that some educators are willing to accept the word of less well-informed peripheral "specialists." Publishers, for example, often find easy access to the classroom for their materials and techniques regardless of research findings. One famous publisher of reading materials sells a spelling package that is really only a vocabulary kit. He knows it because the research tells him so. But a spelling package is a better seller, and many educators do not ask questions.

The research problem starts right at the beginning of reading instruction, where many traditional practices have no basis in empirical research. For example, basal reading systems insist that a sight vocabulary of 50, 75, or 100 words is necessary before teaching word-attack skills. There is no substantial evidence calling for this requirement. Some basal systems teach sight vocabulary before letter knowledge, but research indicates that letter names can be taught long before a child masters 75 words. (20)

Reading-readiness training is an excellent example of the poor use of research. How much time does a school spend on reading-readiness exercises consisting of language development through pictures, non-word forms, motor skills, non-word sounds? Usually the studies show from .05 to .30 correlations between reading-readiness scores and reading achievement in grade 1. (2;6;13;21) On the other hand, research suggests that letter knowledge, training in auditory discrimination of sounds in words, and visual perception of words correlate approximately .65 with reading achievement. (17;18) Despite this evidence, many schools continue to spend disproportionate amounts of time on traditional reading-readiness exercises.

Much has been said lately in and out of the profession about the content of basal readers. Most of the discontent has no basis in empirical data. Are high-interest, low-vocabulary books better teachers of reading than basal readers? Generally speaking, no, according to Anna Harris's research. (14) One textbook publisher has invested large sums to color the skin of characters in his basal reader. People in some professions feel that basal readers are culturally distant from city-dwelling, disadvantaged children. But no convincing data have shown that shading the skin of characters in book illustrations makes a difference in self-concept or in reading achievement.

The problem is twofold: many professional educators neglect existing research; and they also neglect to ask questions about their own practices. In other words, the educator must not only apply some of the "truths" of research, but he should, himself, implement research. He should not use a technique unless he has some evidence that a particular practice works. Furthermore, he must discover if his technique works better than other techniques. This tall order is, at best, only partially filled, but it is a guideline to administrative decisions on quantity and quality of learning.

SUMMARY OF SPECIFIC PROBLEMS

Three specific problems face educators who attempt to increase the quantity and quality of learning. First, we must solve the problem of educating individuals in a system of mass schooling: we must match *content* to various individual needs; we must adjust *levels of* instruction to individual capacities and achievements; we must adjust *speed* of teaching to rate of learning for each individual; and we must insure that every individual is *actively participating* in a learning experience and not waiting to participate. We must do this without relying on a traditional tutorial system.

The second specific problem involves "quality." We have not sufficiently defined "quality of learning." As a result, we have not refined methodology to increase quality. Feedback from the realities of everyday life, in every area of social stress, tells us that Christian ethics, democracy, respect for individual rights, and a sense of social responsibility—stated goals of the American school—have not been adequately taught.

The third problem in upgrading learning involves research. Educational practices have not kept pace with educational research. Furthermore, many educators lack a favorable attitude to research and allow certain traditional assumptions about teaching and learning to exist without adequate evidence of their validity.

§   Some Solutions

The first job of the educator is to increase the quantity and quality of learning in the schools. If he is to affect youth and community, he will do it best by fulfilling his unique professional function. He will improve the technology of teaching by building a methodology based on research. Such a methodology will be geared to individualizing content, level, speed, and frequency of involvement in active learning. *What guidelines will he use to build his technology?*

Goodwin Watson has published a pamphlet in which he lists fifty psychological propositions that "we can trust." (24) They have withstood competition on science's open market of experimentation. Hillgard gives a condensed list of learning propositions that most theorists will support. (15:486) Both lists are convenient guides to building sound methodologies for the classroom.

As an example of sound methodology, let us consider a reading program built according to those learning principles we can trust. Then let us examine the psychosocial implications of such a methodology.

A Sketch of a Model Reading Program

Reading is one skill we expect every normal child to acquire. An ideal reading program includes systematic instruction in *every* subskill of reading arranged in a hierarchy of complexity. The core of this program would include a "least common denominator" of skills for every student.

On the basis of a detailed diagnosis, each student begins the core program at his appropriate "need level." He proceeds at his own pace. Remediation, extra instruction, and enrichment supplement this program. The modes of instruction are as varied as there are materials and techniques in the educator's repertoire. The teacher is part of the core and the supplementary programs. His job is to be one mode of teaching as well as the over-all supervisor who matches materials and techniques to individual needs.

For example, at Mobilization for Youth, we are working on oral-aural-visual-writing techniques for teaching reading to illiterate and semiliterate school dropouts. We hope, eventually, to modify this for every grade level. We are considering a core developmental program built around a ten-station language lab and programmed books. Other programs will supplement the core program: for example, we can collect and collate existing materials and adapt them to self-directing, self-correcting teaching aids. All such materials will be adapted for use by individuals or by learning teams of ten, five, three, and two. The teacher will weave together this complex of materials and students. He will:

1. Provide conditions for learning by building the "therapeutic classroom atmosphere" in which students risk behavior change.
2. Teach students how to teach themselves.
3. Insure success by carefully matching needs and materials.
4. Diagnose, guide, interpret, and evaluate growth in conjunction with each student, as a service to them, *not* as a judgment.
5. Supply on-the-spot first aid when materials do not work or are unavailable.
6. Develop new materials to solve the same problem in the future.
7. Personally interact with individuals and small groups.
8. Group and continuously regroup small learning teams.
9. Introduce as many enrichment experiences as his creativity allows.

A sound methodology is based on precise definition, perception, and action; the educator must think *operationally*. The term "reading" includes so many operations that it loses its meaning when we try to construct a methodology. When we say that Johnnie cannot discriminate the *bl* blend from other sounds at the beginning of words when they are presented to him aurally, we have reached a useful level of specificity. Now we know exactly what operation Johnnie must learn.

In reading, we must isolate a huge number of these necessary operations. Fortunately, students pick up most of these operations incidentally without direct training. But every student, regardless of capacity and achievement, will have a unique pattern of poorly developed operations that must be improved. This is one reason for individualization of the program.

This presents the educator with a formidable task. He must isolate specific operations in a learning goal, and he must develop materials and techniques so the individual can learn these operations with a minimum of teacher direction. With the help of research, educators can anticipate many of the operations. Meanwhile, in the classroom he will continuously discover or refine more and more specific operations for which he will need to develop new materials. This will be one of the educator's major tasks. Development of materials and techniques is the responsibility of the classroom teacher working in conjunction with supervisors and administrators in regularly scheduled, on-going, in-service staff conferences.

Let us look at an example of a specific skill. Johnnie has worked through the beginning of a program in primary reading. He has learned the alphabet. He can perform a number of auditory and visual perceptions necessary for beginning reading. He is beginning to build a sight vocabulary and some basic phonetic skills. One day, Johnnie discovers that he cannot write from dictation: "Pat put the bag on the bed." The teacher notices that he continues to have trouble with medial short vowel sounds. A two-minute spot test confirms the teacher's suspicion.

The teacher moves Johnnie to a machine programmed with combination tape-card series on auditory and visual discrimination of medial short vowel sounds. Three other classmates need the same training and work with Johnnie in one corner of the room, using headsets to reduce noise and increase concentration. They stay on the machine at half-hour intervals for two hours per day. In two days, two members leave the group because they have mastered the skill. They move on to another operation. Johnnie and his partner continue on a set of three-inch reel tapes with programmed answer booklets, supplemented by exercises from standard workbooks.

In other parts of the room, students are working on other skills. One group of three are reading books they have selected from the classroom library. They could read well when they entered the program. These students will write short descriptions of their stories, or they will read stories to less-advanced students. Four other students are preparing special projects of their own interest. Ten students are proceeding in the language laboratory through the core developmental reading program. Each student works at his own level and rate, on content matched to his needs and/or interests. Everyone is actively learning. No one is waiting for others to catch up. No one is waiting for his next turn. Intensity of learning is high.

How does this methodology match valid laws of learning? (14:486)

1. Capacity affects *who* should learn *what* and *when*. In a private school we might prescribe a course of study and then seek out individuals whose abilities and needs fit the prescription. In this case, the *what* and *when* are given, and we adjust the *who*. But in mass public

education, the *who* is given, and we must adjust the *when* and *what* to meet the capacities and needs of the individuals.

Everyone cannot always learn the same things. Even when they can, they may not be able to learn at the same rate. This is true of rats, chimps, middle-class white children, and students in any country. A rigid, lock-step developmental program in any content area violates this principle. Whatever we decide to teach, the program must be adjustable to individual timetables.

2. "A motivated learner acquires what he learns more readily than one who is not motivated." (*ibid.*) In the previous model, motivation is handled according to valid learning principles:

a. Motivation that is too intense (as in pain, fear, or extreme anxiety) may introduce to learning distracting emotional states. Every youngster recognizes every other classmate's strengths and weaknesses because the methodology is built upon these factors. Johnnie recognizes that he shares a specific weakness with three classmates. He also recognizes that two other classmates working on another skill, in another part of the room, do not have the same weakness. Their problem is different, but they have a problem. Pupils are alternately operating according to their strengths and weaknesses. Individual differences are obvious not only to the teacher but more importantly, to the pupils.

In this system the basis of motivation is need and strength. These are openly apparent to every student. This is a therapeutic atmosphere because each student is able to bare his weakness and to correct it. Instead of punishing Johnnie for his weaknesses, the school rewards

Johnnie for helping discover his own weakness and for remedying that weakness. Ego defense is unnecessary.

Finally, the system provides a floating teacher who can boost the ego of the threatened child and control the level of motivation.

b. Learning under intrinsic motivation is preferable to learning under extrinsic motivation. The entire program is built on achievement rewards; that is, not on grades or candy, but on successful achievement of a skill, which becomes thereafter the basic motivation. Research indicates that achievement is its own reward and stimulates the subject to further achievement. Every normal youngster wants to succeed.

c. Success—or positive—reward is preferable to failure or punishment—negative reward. Research shows that target behavior in the laboratory tends to be learned equally as well with positive or negative reinforcers. However, most learning specialists agree that side effects or "social byproducts" (non-target behavior) are more favorable when learning is reinforced positively.

In the model program, failure or lack of success is a temporary state. The goal is success; the methodology offers each individual the chance to succeed.

d. "Tolerance for failure is best taught through providing a backlog of success that compensates for experienced failure." (*ibid.*) By focusing on strengths and weaknesses and on specific operations, the teacher can match materials to strengths to insure success, and then to weaknesses to insure growth. If learning goals are defined operationally in very specific subskills, the individuals can move step by step through a complex pattern with high incidence of success. This is the most valuable feature of programmed instruction. Success is built in so strongly that it compensates for occasional failure. When it does not, the model program provides a floating teacher who can aid the individual, because all of his time is not monopolized by the whole class.

3. "Individuals need practice in setting goals for themselves, goals neither so low as to elicit little effort nor so high as to foreordain to failure. Realistic goal-setting leads to more satisfactory improvement than unrealistic goal-setting." (*ibid.*) In the model program, instruction is largely self-directing. The individual student is constantly making decisions. He constantly checks and paces himself. His teacher is a consultant who offers suggestions for goals and for means. But it is the individual who discovers for himself that he cannot write "Pat put the bag on the bed." And it is the individual who seeks help with medial short vowels.

4. "Active participation by a learner is preferable to passive reception." (*ibid.*) The model program's primary feature is high-intensity learning. Frequency of response is high because instruction is individualized. The program incorporates this feature of a tutorial system, while preserving the advantages of a group experience, by using self-teaching materials individually or in learning teams. The student does the teaching in conjunction with materials, classmates, and a supervising teacher.

5. Meaningful tasks are learned more efficiently than tasks

not understood by the learner. In the model program this learning principle partially is fulfilled through a sixth principle:

6. "Information about the nature of a good performance, knowledge of his own mistakes, and knowledge of successful results aid learning." (*ibid.*) Many educators insist that all materials should relate directly to the student's needs or interests. So, for example, they argue that basal reader content is relatively meaningless to culturally deprived youngsters who cannot relate to the middle-class content. This is an excellent guiding principle: The materials and tasks of the model program should conform to the student's needs or interests.

However, there are other types of meaning. This is implied in our research, which indicates, for example, that basal readers are as effective as "high interest" literature in teaching reading. Knowledge of one's strengths and weaknesses, knowledge of the nature and reason for a task, knowledge of goals, knowledge of results of drill exercises, and the chance to succeed give these tasks and materials tremendous meaning for individuals who want to succeed.

A good learning program uses both types of meaning to promote learning.

7. "The personal history of the individual, for example, his reaction to authority, may hamper or enhance his ability to learn from a given teacher." (*ibid.*) I hope the day will come when teachers and administrators are psychologically secure enough to recognize individual differences, of temperament and perception and are willing to transfer youngsters in order to best match teacher-student personalities. Meanwhile, a teaching

program that allows both maximum and minimum contact between teacher and student will help us adjust
to this problem. Under the model program, a youngster
who cannot relate to his teacher (or vice versa) can
benefit from self-teaching programs and from close
personal interaction with his classmates in learning
teams.

*What are the psychosocial implications of such a
methodology?* The model program tries to add the advantages of tutorial instruction to the techniques of mass
education. It does not replace large-group teaching entirely.
Whatever values exist in a teacher talking to or at thirty
people at once can still be retained. But in implementing
a methodology based on individual self-instruction or small-
team learning, we make some important decisions about the
type of persons we graduate from our schools.

Social responsibility: If four youngsters sit in a tight
cluster with headsets plugged into one Bell and Howell
Language Master, they are forced to operate in close har-
mony to achieve their goals. The programs in phonics that
we are building into these machines require complex processes which depend upon cooperative effort. Team-learning
techniques to teach skills and content thrust youngsters
into situations in which they must depend upon each other.
Our preliminary research with machines and team learning
shows that when youngsters choose to work on a skill, they
quickly master the technology of the machine and recognize
the necessity of interdependence. Research at Boston University shows higher achievement on many tasks and in
content units that are self-taught in teams of two, three, five,
or ten than when taught in groups of thirty or individually. (25)

To teach social responsibility, I prefer the real to the vicarious learning experience. In team learning, social responsibility is necessary to reach individual goals. It is taught incidentally. Incidental learning is a subtle and potent technique because it is not artificial and cannot easily be resisted since it is largely unconscious.

Personal responsibility: A self-directing, self-correcting learning experience requires the individual to make decisions. He must teach himself. This is not a structureless situation. Like most areas of our daily lives, this is a highly structured environment, but the structure provides for adequate amounts of self-direction.

Positive self-direction and decision making are two characteristics of maturity. Producing mature individuals is one of the school's goals. Yet, under present methodology education contributes to the "social prolongation of infancy" by spoon-feedings, tight schedules, restrictions, dormitory curfews, etc. (16:67) From kindergarten through graduate and professional school, students are told what, when, how much, and by what means to read. I have never become accustomed to the look of panic on the faces of my college students right up to the doctoral level when I refuse to assign a textbook for a course.

Social-personal development: In a program geared to individual needs, each youngster can perceive himself as successful; he can sense his own worth. Furthermore, he can recognize the variety of strengths and weaknesses in his classmates. In the model classroom, individuality is a reality, not a glittering generality. Materials and methods are matched to the student, not he to them. With everyone working at his own pace on his own needs, he can devote time to some of his special interests—to what we call "pupil specialties." They become part of the classroom routine. Suddenly, his interests are important to the school; it is as if the culture were saying, "We recognize and respect your uniqueness."

Rewards and satisfactions: Today's schools talk about the evils of materialism, while at the same time over their student's heads as enticements to achieve they hold extrinsic rewards; for example, grades, honors, prizes, special privileges. In contrast, the model program focuses on intrinsic rewards: success in achievement is its own reward. The program offers the school the distinction of being the only social institution to revitalize a noble ideal. The possible social consequences would be certainly worth the educational effort to decrease extrinsic reinforcement and promote intrinsic reward.

General hostility and negative behavior: If theories of individual and social behavior are valid, negatively reinforced behavior affects the total personality in areas beyond the specific behavior being learned. The social by-products of constant negative reinforcement are hostility and, in general, negative behavior throughout the entire personality. The model program uses positive reinforcement and avoids these negative social by-products.

Frustration tolerance: When the school provides an atmosphere for success, it is building for the personality a foundation of success that will withstand occasional failure. In culturally deprived areas, if the public school would develop the methodological style of the model program, it could be the major social force dedicated to building reserves of success in a population that usually experiences failure, rejection, and disapproval. The juvenile delinquency in disadvantaged areas may be a result of this frustration of repeated failure.

Control of destiny: One of the salient characteristics of

culturally deprived youngsters (and oldsters) is the attitude of futility. Actually this characteristic cuts across social classes, but it is more easily concealed in suburbia. Puerto Ricans on East 2nd Street or Negroes on 125th Street feel no hope for tomorrow because they are helpless victims of today's conditions. In a self-directing learning process, the individual can become partial master of his educational destiny. The school has an obligation to give every individual the chance to taste this mastery.

SUMMARY OF SOME SOLUTIONS

To increase the quality and quantity of learning, we must individualize instruction. The school must offer a program of self-directed learning based on reliable principles.

I have briefly sketched a model program for the teaching of reading and have redefined the teacher's role in this program. I have selected some of the reliable laws of learning which can be applied to classroom methodology.

Finally, I have presented some psychosocial implications of this methodology. I suspect that in the school, methodology more than content is the key to effecting social change. This is the basis of my contention: when the educator assumes his core function, he will make his greatest contribution to his community.

§ Conclusions

We may talk with good intentions about educational technology, but the true value of intentions is action. Have educators' actions been compatible with their intentions? Let us look at our methodology.

We may say we believe in individuality, but we focus

thirty pairs of eyes on the same page of the same reader used next door, across town, and in a distant state. We strive for equal expenditure of public funds for every child, but some children need more facilities, more services, more opportunities to learn in order to achieve self-actualization. There would appear to be an inconsistency between what the schools may say they want to do and what the schools are, in fact, doing.

For this reason I have tried to restate and simplify: (1) the unique role of professional educators, (2) some specific problems we must solve to fulfill that role, (3) some guidelines for action and a methodological model. The goals of educators that I learned in graduate school and that I have read in stated philosophies of school systems in which I have taught have not been achieved in fact, because methodology has been inconsistent with this unique role. I have illustrated my case in terms of reading instruction because it is my current specialty and because it is so basic to formal schooling. My concern, however, goes beyond the reading classroom.

I have seen the faces of the unemployed in the cities. That same expression clouds the faces of semiliterate adolescents who attend our reading clinic at a state reform school for delinquent boys. That same look of futility and helplessness marks a population of New York's Lower East Side. Even "privileged" adolescents who enjoy the so-called comforts of suburbia sometimes feel the despair and absurdity of an alienated existence. They sense that the world of school has a double standard, one represented by its words and one reflected in its methodology.

The issue of the educator's role, the problems of methodology, and the guidelines for action are my attempts to effect a means of educating young people. I hope that the school will reverse itself, pull away from present social trends, and assume its basic obligations to improve both the quality and quantity of learning. To do so, educators must move in the methodological direction suggested in this paper. When they do, the school will become a great social force for the preservation of the individual.

Notes

1. David A. Abramson, "The Achievement in College of High-Ability Students Who Had Been in Special Classes and Special School while in High School." Unpublished Ed.D. thesis, New York University, School of Education, 1958.

2. Ruth J. Allen, et al. "The Relationship of Readiness Factors to January First-Grade Reading Achievement." Unpublished Master's thesis, Boston University, 1959.

3. Mary Austin, et al. The Torchlighters. Cambridge, Mass.: Harvard University Press, 1961.

4. Mayvis L. Baumann, "Differing Instructional Needs for Children of Similar Reading Achievement, Grades 2, 4, 6." Unpublished Master's thesis, Boston University, 1960.

5. Marcia E. Berg, "Reading Problems of the Bottom Third, Grades 1-6." Unpublished Master's thesis, Boston University, 1961.

6. Mary A. Blessington, "A Study of the Relationship Between Success on the Drawing of the Diamond and Success in Reading." Unpublished Master's thesis, Boston University, 1950.

7. Leonard Bloomfield and Clarence L. Barnhart, Let's Read: A Linguistic Approach. Detroit: Wayne State University, 1961.

8. Theodore Brameld, Toward a Reconstructed Philosophy of Education. New York: Holt, Rinehart & Winston, Inc., 1956.

9. Hobert W. Bruns and Charles J. Brauner, Philosophy of Education. New York: The Ronald Press Company, 1962.

10. Bruce Dearing, "Three Myths about the College Teacher," The Saturday Review (January 18, 1964), p. 65.

11. John Dewey, The School and Society. Chicago: University of Chicago Press, 1902.

12. Ruth B. Eckstrom, Experimental Studies of Homogeneous

Grouping: A Review of the Literature. Princeton, N.J.: Educational Testing Service, 1959.

13. Florence P. Genua, "The Construction and Validation of an Instrument to Measure the Background Experience of First-Grade Children." Unpublished Ed.D. thesis, Boston University, 1954.

14. Anna S. Harris, "The Relationship Between Reading Progress and Materials Used in the Teaching of Reading to Retarded Readers in Grades 4, 5, and 6." Unpublished Ph.D. thesis, New York University, 1962.

15. Ernest R. Hilgard, *Theories of Learning.* New York: Appleton-Century-Crofts, Inc., 1956.

16. Horace M. Kallen, *The Education of Free Men.* New York: Farrar, Straus & Co., Inc., 1949.

17. Helen Murphy, "An Evaluation of Exercises for Developing Auditory Discrimination in Beginning Reading." Unpublished Master's thesis, Boston University, 1949.

18. ———. "An Evaluation of the Effect of Specific Training in Auditory and Visual Discrimination on Beginning Reading." Unpublished Ed.D. thesis, Boston University, 1943.

19. *The New York Times*, January 26, 1964, "News Notes," p. E9.

20. Arthur V. Olson, "Growth in Word Perception as It Relates to Success in Beginning Reading." Unpublished Ed.D. thesis, Boston University, 1957.

21. Alta M. Saunders, "The Relationship of Certain Readiness Factors to Achievement in Beginning Reading." Unpublished Master's thesis, Boston University, 1947.

22. Arthur S. Trace, *What Ivan Knows That Johnny Doesn't.* New York: Random House, Inc., 1961.

23. Charles C. Walcutt, (ed.). *Tomorrow's Illiterates.* Boston: Little, Brown & Company, 1961.

24. Goodwin Watson, *What Psychology Can We Trust?* New York: Bureau of Publications, Teachers College, Columbia University, 1961.

25. S. Edward Weinswig, "Evaluation of Lessons to Teach Map Skills in Grade 4." Unpublished Ed.D. thesis, Boston University, 1962.

26. For a report on seventeen studies in pupil-team learning, see *Journal of Education*, CXLVI, No. 2 (December, 1963), pp. 42-44.

6

ADMINISTRATIVE IMPLICATIONS OF INTEGRATION PLANS FOR SCHOOLS

OPEN ENROLLMENT IN NEW YORK CITY

**Eleanor Bernert Sheldon, James R. Hudson
and Raymond A. Glazier**

§ Introduction

To be of value to the administrator, social science efforts and findings must be translated so as to provide information that can be injected into the process of administrative decision making. We hope to bring together here some social science conceptualizations and findings that may have application in and implication for administrative decision making in public school systems of large urban centers.

An analysis of conflict situations is particularly important in this context. Subsumed under this broad canopy we might draw upon three heuristic approaches: (1) the means-ends schema, (2) the expectation-perception schema drawn from role theory, and (3) a social change model. These approaches are neither mutually exclusive nor exhaustive, nor are they independent of each other. In the following discussion of some current conflicts in many northern central city school systems, understanding is sought from all three conceptual standpoints.

Conflicts between groups of interacting persons in the school system are of prime importance in this connection. Here we are particularly concerned with the internal group (defined for our purposes as the board of education and/or superintendent) and external groups (parental, civil rights, and other groups).[1] The social science problem becomes one of delineating and defining conflicts, postulating their causes, and operationalizing this theoretical analysis into an empirical research program and then deriving administrative implications from research findings. For the present, in the absence of a completed research program, if we can derive hypotheses that may explain the bases of the conflict, they may prove of some value to administrative decision making.

We must postulate a conflict or disparity if not in ultimate goals, at least in the more proximate objectives and/or means of achieving them in the relationship between components of the educational system—in our instance, a board of education and/or superintendent vis-à-vis the clients. To deny the existence of a conflict with respect to the objectives or the obtaining means would be to deny the existence of problems.[2]

We view schools as institutions specifically invested with a service function—the moral and technical socialization of the young. The direct clients of the service function are, of course, the pupils.[3] The indirect clients comprise the parental groups, the public, and similar groups. At times either one or both of the client societies may be characterized by values (goals) which are at best irrelevant to the service goals of the school and often opposed to them. Coleman's more recent study and an earlier one by Gordon, for example, indicate that student subcultures center on non-academic values, such as athletics and dating.[4] In such instances the school structure and modes of operation must be adapted to meet the exigencies occasioned by the value differences. Schools in pursuit of achieving their service function (the production, at least at a minimum level for elementary and junior high schools, of a uniform product for adult citizenship) are affected by: (1) professional standards of teachers and administrators, (2) client (direct and indirect) desires and pressures, and (3) fiscal efficiency —the last often performing as the balancing mechanism of the first two.

The goals of schools tend to be stated at best in diffuse terms, but they must be specified in terms of intermediate objectives before they become the ends of action. For example, the New York City Integration Plan, dated August 23, 1963, stated its goal as follows:

> In the years since the historic 1954 decision of the United States Supreme Court, and even earlier, the New York City Public Schools have pursued earnestly their commitment to the objective of racial integration in the schools. Much has been accomplished. Nevertheless our midsummer 1963 stock-taking makes it clear that much more has to be done. Our past programs and activities were appropriate for their time, but we now propose to embark on a new series of endeavors which we hope will hasten the day when our city is completely integrated and all of our children will enjoy equal educational opportunity. We believe that school integration is an important part of our pursuit of excellence for all children.[5]

The plan then went on to present a rather detailed outline of four major fronts of attack: (1) moral, (2) desegregation, (3) instructional, and (4) job. The program of open enrollment represents one of seven facets of the desegregation front; included among the others are zoning changes and recruitment of more Negro and Puerto Rican teachers.

With increasing specificity there is a tendency to add intermediate objectives, to modify or change the ends, and to establish a set of priorities. The occasion for priorities generally arises in adverse situations where scarce resources make it impossible for the organization to achieve all its goals simultaneously. By December 28, 1963, for example, the Board of Education was forced to re-emphasize that a constructive integration plan must embrace two "essential goals—ethnic distribution and quality education." In addition, at this time the distinction was made between *segregation* (the result of a deliberate effort of exclusion) and *ethnic distribution* (the result of housing patterns). The Board suggested that *integration* in New York City in 1963 is fundamentally an educational program in contrast to *desegregation* in some parts of the country which is a matter of correcting past injustices growing out of the deliberate efforts of exclusion.[6] A plan proposed in 1964 provided for more specific objectives and priorities.[7] Some of the problems confronting the New York City school system and many other northern urban school systems exemplify this process of increasing specificity, adversity in implementation and subsequent modification.

The primary goal of a school system is to produce an acceptable educational level by developing the intellectual, technical, and the moral wherewithal for adult life. The school system as part of a larger society is also being affected by the two major social revolutions of the day—the technological revolution involving automation of skills and the Negro "revolution" involving demands for rights. These major social trends impinge upon the operations of the school system (1) where the objectives of professional standards and client pressures may differ, (2) where objectives might be similar though the means of obtaining them may differ, and (3) where both the ends and the means differ. In the event of divergence in means (2) and (3), fiscal feasibility and efficiency often interferes with obtaining the stated ends, usually resulting again in greater specificity and priority of the proximate objectives.

The internal school system must adapt sufficiently to achieve a workable level of client satisfaction while maintaining its service function. Client satisfaction is affected by: (1) the expectations by which clients define the role of members of a board of education and/or superintendent and (2) their perceptions of the behavior of the incumbents of these roles. With respect to (1), role expectations define appropriate administrative behavior; and with respect to (2), perceptions of that behavior serve to evaluate the role behavior.

The convergence or divergence of these expectations and perceptions defines the degree of conflict: (1) If the board and/or superintendent is perceived as behaving in a way defined as the clients' expectations, then the administrative structure would be positively evaluated. (2) On the other hand, if the behavior is perceived as different from that defined by the expectations, then a negative evaluation can be anticipated. (3) In addition, negative evaluation will arise with respect to differences in expectations.

The relationship between the means-ends approach and the expectation-perception schema is clear. Convergence of expectations and perceptions can be equated with similarity or even identity of objectives and means on the part of the school system and the client. This, of course, provides peace.

Differences between perceived behavior and expected behavior correspond to a situation where there may be similarity of goals and intermediate objectives, but conflict over the obtaining means. Differences in expectations can be viewed as differences in objectives.

Perhaps little is added to the means-ends approach by the imposition of role-theory concepts. In viewing, however, particular crisis situations, which in New York City arise when the broad abstract goals become specific proximate objectives and hierarchically ordered, the expectation-perception approach may assist in avoiding the hazards of becoming involved in the complexities resulting from the concomitant realignment of ends and means.

Introducing the classical model of social change has the advantage of leading us into the descriptive phrases of what is currently happening in New York City.[8] The model we have in mind derives from the idealized version of stages in population growth: (1) the static stage—population change is relatively slow, allowing for adaptation of institutions; (2) the dynamic transitional stage—population change is marked, making for a lag in institutional adaptation; and (3) static stage following the revolution—population change levels out, allowing institutional adjustment to catch up. (see Figure 1.) Such a model was originally developed and has since proved useful in examining demographic changes, particularly in industrializing nations. It has application also, however, in examining population shifts currently affecting many of this nation's institutions and finding its most precipitant effect in school systems of large urban centers.

The nation's agrarian past is finished; and the heart of our country rests in great cities. The changing population structure of our metropolitan communities is one of the

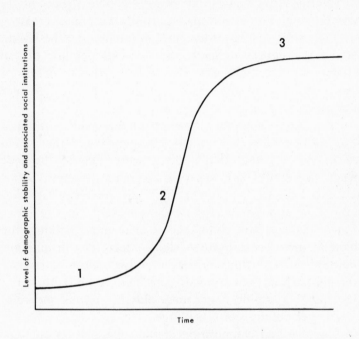

Figure 1—Social Change Model

most consequential social phenomena of the current age. Most of us are acquainted with its general features:

The shift of population in the United States is to metropolitan areas. The concomitant movement of population from the central cities to the suburbs has also become increasingly pronounced, particularly during the decade of the fifties. Metropolitan concentration and suburban dispersal themselves, however, are perhaps less significant than the sorting-out process that is changing markedly the social and economic characteristics of the population of central cities and outlying areas.

Central cities seem to be losing long-term residents to the suburbs and replacing them partially with migrants from non-metropolitan areas, often rural migrants from the South. Though the figures indicate only a small net loss of the population of central cities, there has been a high rate of gross migration turnover, differentially (e.g., by age and color) involving large numbers of persons.

Secondary demographic results of these shifts in population residence are seen in the changing population structure of the city and the outlying areas. During the past decade the white population of the nation's central cities increased by only 5 per cent while the crresponding non-white population increased by 51 per cent. In the cities of the Northeast this difference is even more striking, for whites in these central cities actually decreased in number. One result of this ethnic succession in large cities is that the remaining white population is considerably older than the non-white, containing many more elderly persons and relatively fewer children of school age.

The size and composition of these population changes are intimately related to the structure of a city's body politic, the nature and direction of its social change and problems, as well as to the city's possibile avenues of adjustment to change.

§   Demographic and School Enrollment Changes

The 1960 census of New York City shows a small total population decline of about 110,000 persons between 1950 and 1960, from about 7,892,000 to almost 7,782,000. However, this net decline represents the balance of white population loss of about 475,000 and a non-white population increase of approximately 365,000.[9] The city's Puerto Rican population increased almost 150 per cent, from approximately 245,000 in 1950 to almost 615,000 in 1960. The balance of in- and out-migration among whites (excluding Puerto Ricans) resulted in a loss of 1.2 million persons, while the net migration of non-whites and Puerto Ricans resulted in a gain of about 380,000 persons.[10] With the exception of those born during the immediate postwar period (aged 10-14 years in 1960) the age structure of the white population indicates a decline in each five-year age group under 50 years of age with the greatest proportionate declines in the peak productive years, 20-40 years old. Non-white increases, on the other hand, occurred, in each of the age groups, particularly among the preschool and school ages. (See Table 1.)

Table 1—New York City: Age Distribution of Population, by Color, 1950 and 1960, and Per Cent Change 1950 to 1960

| | White Population | | | Non-white Population | | |
| | NUMBER | | | NUMBER | | |
AGE (YEAR)	1950	1960	CHANGE (PER CENT)	1950	1960	CHANGE (PER CENT)
All Ages	7,116,441	6,640,662	—6.7	775,516	1,141,322	47.2
Under 5	587,649	546,341	—7.0	78,240	140,376	79.4
5-9	480,051	479,069	—0.2	54,988	116,778	112.4
10-14	395,131	482,318	22.1	48,468	93,003	91.8
15-19	419,714	417,639	—0.5	47,351	69,212	46.2
20-24	528,325	400,847	—24.1	70,393	81,675	16.0
25-29	576,951	423,310	—26.6	88,294	90,319	2.3
30-34	559,352	443,393	—20.7	78,897	99,376	26 0
35-39	591,483	447,292	—24.4	77,362	99,674	28.8
40-44	577,915	441,286	—23.6	64,150	83,095	29.5
45-49	537,558	478,891	—10.9	53,064	71,419	34.6
50-54	515,331	476,722	—7.5	41,058	57,804	40.8
55-59	424,385	449,792	6.0	26,130	49,701	90.2
60-64	345,577	394,363	11.4	18,905	34,462	82.3
65 and over	577,019	759,399	31.6	28,216	54,428	92.9

Sources: U.S. Bureau of the Census, *Census of Population, 1950*, Vol. 2: *Characteristics of the Population*, Part 32, New York, Table 33, p. 84; *U.S. Census of Population, 1960, General Population Characteristics*, New York, Final Report PC(1)-34B, Table 20, p. 86.

The dispersal of the city's total population throughout its constituent boroughs is indicated in Table 2. Here we see a decline in the percentage of the city's population residing in Manhattan, a concomitant increase in the outlying areas of Queens and the Bronx, and only a little change in Brooklyn and Richmond. A corresponding pattern of dispersal among Negroes is also indicated (Table 3) though the heaviest concentration remains in Manhattan and Brooklyn. While almost 90 per cent of the city's total population resided in Manhattan and Brooklyn in 1900, less than 60 per cent lived in these boroughs in 1950 and only 55 per cent in 1960. Similarly 90 per cent of the Negro population resided in Manhattan and Brooklyn in 1900, 80 per cent in 1950, and 70 per cent in 1960.

Table 2—New York City: Per Cent Distribution of Total Population, by Borough, 1900-1960

Area	PER CENT OF TOTAL POPULATION						
	1960	1950	1940	1930	1920	1910	1900
New York City	100.0	100.0	100.0	100.0	100.0	100.0	100.0
Bronx	18.3	18.4	18.7	18.3	13.0	9.0	5.8
Brooklyn	33.8	34.7	36.2	36.9	35.9	34.3	34.0
Manhattan	21.8	24.8	25.4	26.9	40.7	48.9	53.8
Queens	23.3	19.7	17.4	15.6	8.3	6.0	4.5
Richmond	2.8	2.4	2.3	2.3	2.1	1.8	1.9

Sources: U.S. Bureau of the Census, *U.S. Census of Population, 1960, General Population Characteristics, New York,* Final Report PC(1)-34B, Table 20, p. 86, and Table 27, pp. 156, 162, 165, 168, 169; *Census of Population, 1950,* Vol. 2: *Characteristics of the Population,* Part 32, New York, Table 34, p. 94; *Sixteenth Census of the United States [1940], Population,* Vol. 2: *Characteristics of the Population,* Part 5, New York-Oregon, [New York] Tables, C-36, D-36, E-36, F-36, G-36, H-36, pp. 157, 164, 171, 178, 185, 192; *Fourteenth Census of the United States,* Vol. 2; *Population, 1920: General Report and Analytical Tables,* Table 16, p. 55.

**Table 3—New York City: Per Cent Distribution of Negro
Population, by Borough, 1900-1960**

Area	PER CENT OF NEGRO POPULATION						
	1960	1950	1940	1930	1920	1910	1900
New York City	100.0	100.0	100.0	100.0	100.0	100.0	100.0
Bronx	15.1	13.1	5.1	3.9	3.2	4.5	3.9
Brooklyn	34.1	27.8	23.4	21.0	20.9	24.8	30.4
Manhattan	36.5	51.5	65.2	68.6	71.6	66.0	59.8
Queens	13.4	6.9	5.6	5.7	3.4	3.5	4.3
Richmond	0.9	0.7	0.7	0.8	0.9	1.3	1.8

Sources: See Table 2.

While the total population of the city declined by
about 1 per cent, the school-age population increased by
15 per cent between 1950 and 1960. This increase, however,
was disproportionately felt in the various boroughs (Table
5). The range in the variations went from a 2 per cent increase in Manhattan to about 10 per cent each in Brooklyn and in the Bronx, over 35 per cent in Queens, and about
50 per cent in Richmond. As the total school-age population
dispersed throughout the boroughs, so did its non-white
component, though at markedly greater rates. Non-white
school-age population for the city increased by almost 90
per cent. In Manhattan the increase came to somewhat
less than 30 per cent, in the Bronx it reached 95 per cent,
in Brooklyn almost 115 per cent, in Richmond almost 160
per cent, and in Queens about 280 per cent. Despite the
decade of dispersal, however, the borough of Manhattan
retained its primary position with a school-age population
of over 30 per cent non-white as compared with less than 20
per cent in each of the other boroughs.

Changes in the ethnic composition among those of school age reveal additional marked differentials. For the city as a whole, the school-age population increased by 6 per cent among the whites and over 85 per cent among the non-whites. Comparable figures for the boroughs show marked local differences. For example, while the non-white school-age population in Queens tripled between 1950 and 1960, the white population of the same ages increased by only 26 per cent. In Manhattan the white school-age population increased by slightly more than 5 per cent, while the non-whites experienced an increase of almost 30 per cent.

Table 4—New York City: Per Cent Distribution of the Population by Age, Color, and Borough, 1950 and 1960

Per Cent of Population

AREA AND AGE (YEARS)	TOTAL		WHITE		NON-WHITE	
	1950	1960	1950	1960	1950	1960
New York City						
All ages	100.0	100.0	100.0	100.0	100.0	100.0
Under 5	8.4	8.8	8.3	8.2	10.1	12.3
5-19	18.3	21.4	18.2	20.8	19.5	24.4
20-44	40.7	33.5	39.8	32.4	48.9	39.8
45-64	24.9	25.9	25.6	27.1	17.9	18.7
65 and over	7.7	10.4	8.1	11.5	3.6	4.8
Bronx						
All ages	100.0	100.0	100.0	100.0	100.0	100.0
Under 5	8.3	8.9	8.1	8.4	11.0	12.6
5-19	19.9	22.1	19.7	21.4	23.0	26.7
20-44	39.3	32.4	38.7	31.5	47.0	39.6
45-64	25.2	25.9	25.9	27.1	16.0	17.1
65 and over	7.3	10.7	7.6	11.6	3.0	4.0

Table 4—Continued

Per Cent of Population

AREA AND AGE (YEARS)	TOTAL		WHITE		NON-WHITE	
	1950	1960	1950	1960	1950	1960
Brooklyn						
All ages	100.0	100.0	100.0	100.0	100.0	100.0
Under 5	9.0	9.6	8.8	8.8	11.7	14.2
5-19	19.8	22.8	19.6	22.1	22.1	26.5
20-44	40.5	33.3	39.9	32.0	47.9	40.7
45-64	23.3	24.5	23.9	26.1	15.0	15.2
65 and over	7.4	9.8	7.8	11.0	3.3	3.4
Manhattan						
All ages	100.0	100.0	100.0	100.0	100.0	100.0
Under 5	7.1	7.6	6.6	6.6	8.9	10.4
5-19	14.6	17.2	14.0	16.0	17.1	20.9
20-44	42.6	35.4	40.6	34.1	50.1	39.3
45-64	27.0	27.5	28.8	29.1	19.9	22.8
65 and over	8.7	12.3	10.0	14.2	4.0	6.6
Queens						
All ages	100.0	100.0	100.0	100.0	100.0	100.0
Under 5	9.1	8.7	9.0	8.3	10.4	12.3
5-19	18.7	21.8	18.6	21.4	19.8	26.1
20-44	40.1	33.1	39.9	32.5	47.7	40.1
45-64	25.0	26.8	25.3	27.7	18.2	17.4
65 and over	7.1	9.6	7.2	10.1	3.9	4.1
Richmond						
All ages	100.0	100.0	100.0	100.0	100.0	100.0
Under 5	10.0	10.2	9.7	10.1	11.0	14.3
5-19	20.5	26.8	21.0	26.3	24.7	34.9
20-44	39.4	32.5	39.2	32.2	43.5	33.8
45-64	22.0	21.3	22.0	21.8	16.4	13.2
65 and over	8.1	9.2	8.1	9.6	4.4	3.8

Sources: U.S. Bureau of the Census, *U.S. Census of Population, 1960, General Population Characteristics, New York,* Final Report PC(1)-34B, Table 20, p. 86; Census of Population, 1950, Vol. 2: *Characteristics of the Population,* Part 32, New York, Tables 33 and 41.

Table 5—New York City: Per Cent Change in Population of Selected Age Groups, by Color and Borough, from 1950 to 1960

AREA AND AGE (YEARS)	PER CENT CHANGE, FROM 1950 TO 1960		
	Total	White	Non-white
New York City			
All ages	—1.4	—6.7	47.0
Under 5	3.2	—7.1	79.5
5-19	14.9	6.5	87.4
20-44	—18.7	—24.0	19.8
45-64	2.6	—1.3	53.2
65 and over	34.5	31.5	92.8
Bronx			
All ages	—1.8	—7.1	69.0
Under 5	5.8	—2.8	90.9
5-19	8.7	1.1	95.7
20-44	—18.9	—24.4	42.6
45-64	0.8	—2.8	81.2
65 and over	43.4	41.7	133.3
Brooklyn			
All ages	—4.0	—11.0	78.9
Under 5	2.0	—10.8	116.0
5-19	10.4	0.4	114.9
20-44	—21.3	—28.7	52.0
45-64	1.2	—2.8	81.2
65 and over	27.6	25.5	85.7
Manhattan			
All ages	—13.4	—18.2	5.4
Under 5	—7.9	—18.4	22.2
5-19	2.1	—6.4	29.0
20-44	—27.9	—31.2	—17.3
45-64	—11.7	—17.8	21.2
65 and over	21.6	16.1	75.0
Queens			
All ages	16.7	10.6	187.8
Under 5	11.3	2.2	242.3
5-19	37.2	26.5	279.3

Table 5—Continued

AREA AND AGE (YEARS)	PER CENT CHANGE, FROM 1950 TO 1960		
	Total	White	Non-white
20-44	—3.5	—9.9	141.6
45-64	25.0	20.8	175.1
65 and over	58.2	54.6	201.4
Richmond			
All ages	15.9	13.9	82.5
Under 5	19.4	16.7	136.9
5-19	51.2	47.2	158.4
20-44	—4.6	—6.1	41.9
45-64	11.9	11.2	47.1
65 and over	32.6	32.3	53.8

Sources: See Source note for Table 4.

What impact have changes in the size and distribution of the population and changes in ethnic composition had upon the city's school enrollments?

First, it should be noted that there have been increases in the size of the parochial and private school enrollments in the city. Between 1957 and 1961 non-public school enrollment increased by about 6 per cent, from 387,000 to 411,000. The increase was greater at the high school grades (over 14 per cent) in contrast to the elementary school grades (about 5 per cent). In the city as a whole, there was a decline in the kindergarten non-public school enrollment. The largest increases in non-public school enrollment occurred in the private and parochial high schools of Queens—where enrollments increased consistently from 9,000 in 1957 to 13,000 in 1961—over 44 per cent. (In 1955 this pupil register amounted to only 6,000 and has increased by more than 115 per cent since that time.) [11]

It appears that the private and parochial schools of the city are absorbing just about their proportional share of increased enrollments—accounting for approximately 30 per cent of the total enrollment in the city during each of these years (about one-third in the elementary schools, something less than 20 per cent in the high schools, and about 15 per cent in the kindergarten register). Unfortunately there are no data currently available on the color and ethnic distribution of non-public school registers. However, 1960 census data indicate that over a third of the white elementary-school children are in private schools, as compared with 8 per cent of the non-white pupils at this level. Twenty-five per cent of the city's white high school pupils are in private schools as compared with 7 per cent among the non-whites. Corresponding figures for kindergarten enrollments are over 20 per cent for whites and 5 per cent for non-whites.[12]

The picture in the city's public schools is strikingly different. From 1957-1958 to 1963-1964 the total public school enrollment increased from 953,000 to close to 1,040,-000—an increase of 9 per cent. The number of Negroes on public school registers between these two dates increased by 92,000, or 53 per cent. Puerto Ricans increased by 49,000, or 38 per cent. The remaining population, which is largely white, experienced a decline in numbers of almost 55,000, or 8 per cent. These changes differed notably at the various school levels and also markedly among the various boroughs (see Tables 6 and 7).

Table 6—New York City: Per Cent Distribution of Enrollment in Public
Schools by Ethnic Group, School Level, and Borough, 1957-1958
and 1963-1964

AREA AND ETHNIC GROUP	ALL SCHOOLS		ELEMENTARY		JUNIOR HIGH		ACADEMIC HIGH		VOCATIONAL HIGH	
	1957-1958	1963-1964	1957-1958	1963-1964	1957-1958	1963-1964	1957-1958	1963-1964	1957-1958	1963-1964
New York City										
Total	100.0	100.0	100.0	100.0	100.0	100.0	100.0	100.0	100.0	100.0
Negro	18.2	25.5	20.5	28.7	18.9	26.9	9.3	14.7	23.6	25.9
Puerto Rican	13.5	17.1	15.3	19.8	16.1	17.9	4.6	7.2	20.4	22.5
Other	68.3	57.4	64.2	51.5	65.0	55.2	86.1	78.1	56.0	51.6
Bronx										
Total	100.0	100.0	100.0	100.0	100.0	100.0	100.0	100.0	100.0	100.0
Negro	15.6	23.6	17.1	25.7	14.7	24.6	9.5	15.0	25.8	25.9
Puerto Rican	19.8	28.1	22.6	32.2	21.2	27.9	6.5	12.3	35.9	42.7
Other	64.6	48.3	60.3	42.1	64.1	47.5	84.0	72.7	38.3	31.4
Brooklyn										
Total	100.0	100.0	100.0	100.0	100.0	100.0	100.0	100.0	100.0	100.0
Negro	17.5	27.0	21.0	31.1	16.7	28.9	7.4	13.1	24.0	27.8
Puerto Rican	10.2	15.5	12.2	18.6	11.5	16.1	2.4	4.9	16.0	20.6
Other	72.3	57.5	66.8	50.3	71.8	55.0	90.2	82.0	60.0	51.6
Manhattan										
Total	100.0	100.0	100.0	100.0	100.0	100.0	100.0	100.0	100.0	100.0
Negro	32.7	38.6	35.7	41.6	33.7	39.7	24.3	31.5	24.8	28.6
Puerto Rican	30.4	31.6	33.6	35.3	34.0	32.8	16.9	20.1	24.0	26.2
Other	36.9	29.8	30.7	23.1	32.3	27.5	58.8	48.4	51.2	45.2
Queens										
Total	100.0	100.0	100.0	100.0	100.0	100.0	100.0	100.0	100.0	100.0
Negro	10.9	17.4	12.4	20.5	12.5	18.1	5.1	9.2	16.8	19.6
Puerto Rican	1.4	2.1	1.7	2.2	1.5	2.1	0.7	1.1	2.8	7.0
Other	87.7	80.5	85.9	77.3	86.0	79.8	94.2	89.7	80.4	73.4
Richmond										
Total	100.0	100.0	100.0	100.0	100.0	100.0	100.0	100.0	100.0	100.0
Negro	6.2	7.8	7.1	8.9	......	9.6	2.6	3.8	12.0	9.3
Puerto Rican	1.4	2.1	1.7	2.2	......	2.4	0.6	1.4	1.8	4.6
Other	92.4	90.1	91.2	88.9	......	88.0	96.8	94.8	86.2	86.1

Source: Derived from tabulations supplied by the Board of Education, City of New York.

Table 7—New York City: Per Cent Change in Enrollment of Public Schools by Ethnic Group, School Level, and Borough, from 1957-1958 to 1963-1964

PER CENT CHANGE, FROM 1957-58 TO 1963-64

AREA AND SCHOOL LEVEL	Total	Negro	Puerto Rican	Other
New York City				
All schools	9.1	53.1	37.7	—8.3
Elementary	5.7	47.8	37.3	—15.3
Junior High	22.7	75.0	36.3	4.2
Academic High	9.0	71.4	73.7	—1.2
Vocational High	—1.6	8.1	8.7	—9.4
Bronx				
All schools	10.5	67.9	56.6	—17.4
Elementary	10.8	66.4	58.0	—22.6
Junior High	16.3	94.4	53.4	—13.8
Academic High	6.3	68.2	100.1	—8.0
Vocational High	—7.5	—7.2	9.9	—24.1
Brooklyn				
All schools	11.9	72.6	70.0	—11.0
Elementary	11.5	65.0	69.3	—15.9
Junior High	23.3	113.4	72.5	—5.5
Academic High	4.7	85.6	114.1	—4.9
Vocational High	4.2	20.8	34.2	—10.5
Manhattan				
All schools	—1.2	16.5	2.6	—20.1
Elementary	—4.0	11.8	0.9	—27.8
Junior High	3.8	22.2	0.2	—11.6
Academic High	17.1	51.7	—39.9	—3.8
Vocational High	—23.4	—11.7	—16.4	—32.3
Queens				
All schools	10.4	77.0	59.3	1.4
Elementary	1.9	67.9	35.2	—8.3
Junior High	32.0	90.8	89.2	22.5
Academic High	11.2	101.3	64.0	6.0
Vocational High	77.0	107.0	352.2	61.4

Table 7—Continued

PER CENT CHANGE, FROM 1957-58 TO 1963-64

AREA AND SCHOOL LEVEL	Total	Negro	Puerto Rican	Other
Richmond				
All schools	19.9	50.2	74.6	17.0
Elementary	—3.4	21.0	24.4	—5.8
Junior High	......	......	......	......
Academic High	19.6	72.5	107.5	17.2
Vocational High	—6.3	—27.8	140.0	—6.4

Source: See source note for Table 6.

In the elementary schools Negro enrollments increased by almost 50 per cent, Puerto Ricans by almost 40 per cent, and the remaining category declined by 15 per cent. At the junior high school level pupil enrollments among Negroes increased by 75 per cent, among Puerto Ricans by almost 40 per cent, and by only 4 per cent for others. At the academic high school level Negro and Puerto Rican enrollments increased by over 70 per cent; enrollment for the other pupils decreased by only 1.2 per cent.

The impact of the changing ethnic composition of the city's population and the concomitant dispersion is reflected in the pupil registers for each borough. While the elementary school enrollment in Manhattan declined by almost 4 per cent between 1957-1958 and 1963-1964, it increased from 2 per cent in Queens to 10 per cent in the Bronx and 12 per cent in Brooklyn, and declined by 3 per cent in Richmond. However, Negro elementary school enrollments increased by almost 70 per cent in Queens, approximately 65 per cent in the Bronx and Brooklyn, 20 per cent in Richmond, and only 12 per cent in Manhattan. Corresponding increases among the Puerto Ricans amounted to 70 per cent in Brooklyn, almost 60 per cent in the Bronx, 35 per cent in Queens, 25 per cent in Richmond, and only 1 per cent in Manhattan. The enrollment of white pupils in elementary schools declined by 22 per cent in the Bronx, 16 per cent in Brooklyn, and 28 per cent in Manhattan, 8 per cent in Queens, and 6 per cent in Richmond.

Similar borough enrollment patterns by ethnic groups are also indicated at the junior high schol level. Whereas the number of white pupils at the junior high school level declined in Manhattan, the Bronx, and Brooklyn, it increased in Queens. Negro enrollments at the city's junior high schools increased in all boroughs from 22 per cent in Manhattan to 90 per cent in Queens, 95 per cent in the Bronx, and 113 per cent in Brooklyn. Similarly for the Puerto Rican enrollment: no change in Manhattan, but increases in each of the other boroughs, 53 per cent in the Bronx, 73 per cent in Brooklyn, and 90 per cent in Queens.

It is primarily at the elementary and junior high school levels that the Open Enrollment Program is directed. It is among these groups, then, where the Superintendent and the Board of Education hope to achieve some "ethnic balance" by utilizing a variety of techniques—one of which is the combined Open Enrollment and Free-choice Transfer Program.

§   Open Enrollment Program

The combined effects of the increasing school enrollment of Negroes and Puerto Rican pupils, the decline in public school enrollment among white pupils, the ecological concentration in the residence of color- and ethnic-group populations, and the borough dispersion pattern have resulted in an expected unequal distribution of the total school enrollments in different areas of the city and, of course, in a disproportionate concentration of color- and ethnic-group pupil registers. Such a result is commonly referred to as *de facto* segregation. In addition, there has occurred the usual delay in the construction of new school buildings, occasioning an increase of over-utilization from approximately 35 per cent of the total school buildings in 1958 to 45 per cent in 1961.

In the school year 1957-1958 there were 64 (11 per cent) of the 565 elementary schools in the city with pupil registers that were 90 per cent or more Negro and/or Puerto Rican. By 1963-1964, 23 per cent of the city's 581 elementary schools had enrollments of 90 per cent or more Negro and/ or Puerto Rican. At the junior high school level, 13 per cent of the total 123 schools had enrollments of 85 per cent or more Negro and/or Puerto Rican in 1957-1958 as compared with 23 per cent in 1963-1964. For each of the four major boroughs (Richmond being excluded) there are corresponding increases in the number of elementary and junior high schools that are predominantly Negro and/or Puerto Rican. At the elementary level, schools so classified increased from 28 per cent to 38 per cent during this time span in Manhattan, from 12 to 30 per cent in the Bronx, from 10 to 25 per cent in Brooklyn, and 4 to 10 per cent in Queens. At the junior high school level the corresponding percentage increased from 30 to 42 per cent in Manhattan, from 15 to 30 per cent in the Bronx, from 7 to 22 per cent in Brooklyn, and from 4 to 6 per cent in Queens.

The Board of Education has attempted to tackle both the problem of overcrowding and that of ethnic imbalance.

While the attacks on the two problems are not necessarily the same, they do converge where overcrowding and increased concentration of Negroes and Puerto Ricans coincide. For example, between 1958 and 1963, fifty thousand pupils were transferred from over-utilized schools to under-utilized schools. Aside from relieving the pressures of over-utilization, the program has also "resulted in a more varied ethnic pupil population in the schools to which the pupils were transferred." [13]

To meet the specific problem of concentration of racial and ethnic groups in certain schools, the Board of Education established in 1960 the Open Enrollment Program. Its goal was stated in these words: "The Open Enrollment program was designed to achieve many significant educational values by providing experiences in democratic living and daily opportunities for children, teachers and parents to work with members of various ethnic groups and cultural backgrounds." [14]

The program has been implemented as follows: It is the responsibility of the Central Zoning Unit of the New York City School Board to select schools to be included in the program. Basically two types of schools were selected: sending schools and receiving schools. The sending schools for the elementary program are those that have a 90 per cent Negro and/or Puerto Rican population or those with a population of 90 per cent "others." For the junior high school program two categories of sending schools were adopted: category A, referring to "elementary schools which fed junior high schools having 85 per cent or more Negro and/or Puerto Rican population; [15] and category B, referring to "elementary schools which had 90 per cent or more Negro and/or Puerto Rican population and which fed junior high schools having between 15 per cent and 25 per cent 'other.' " [16] Category B, however, was eliminated early in the program because of lack of space. Receiving schools were defined as "schools with 75 per cent or more 'others' in population and utilized below 90 per cent. However, in schools showing a declining population in the previous years, the utilization determinant was set at 95 per cent rather than 90 per cent." [17]

Participation in the Open Enrollment Program is voluntary. Within the sending schools, pupils are given an application blank that is to be filled out by their parents stating their preference for inclusion or not in the program. The parents may also select the receiving school (with one to four preferences possible) to which they would like to send their child. A list of receiving schools accompanies the application form.

The processing of applications has gone through many changes but the general outlines remain constant. Since space in receiving schools was limited, a priority system was developed. On the elementary level the principal in the sending school was to mark the date and time the application was received before transmitting it to the Central Zoning Unit. Applications for places in junior high schools were sent directly to the Central Zoning Unit and the postmark was used to determine priority. In all cases it is the Central Zoning Unit that assigns the pupils, thereby relieving the local principal of responsibility.

In September, 1960, a pilot program was conducted to assess the feasibility of the Open Enrollment Program. At that time 7,883 applications were distributed in the third, fourth, and fifth grades of sixteen sending schools. All 284 applications received were authorized for transfer; 212 pupils completed transfers to thirty-one receiving schools in October, 1960.

Following the pilot program in 1960, the Open Enrollment Program was put into operation in 1961. From September 1961 to September 1963, 237,501 applications were
distributed for admission to the third, fourth, and fifth
grades and to junior high schools. More than three hundred
elementary schools and sixty junior high scools participated
in the program. Over twenty thousand transfers were requested and approximately fourteen thousand transfer pupils
actually registered at receiving schools. Responses to the
programs varied by school level. The data suggest that
for admission into grades 3, 4, and 5 the proportion of
distributed applications actually requesting transfer was less
than 5 per cent, while the requests for transfer into junior
high schools amounted to about 20 per cent of the applications distributed. For the combined grade levels, less than
10 per cent of the applications distributed resulted in a
requested transfer.[18]

The Open Enrollment Program, including the pilot
program of 1960, ran from September 1960 to February
1964, when it was replaced by the Free-Choice Transfer
Program. Most pupils enrolled under the Open Enrollment
Program have continued in the schools to which they had
been assigned. The Free-Choice Transfer Program can be
viewed as an extension of the Open Enrollment Program.
Under it all schools in the New York City system have been
reviewed as to possible inclusion as a sending or a receiving
school. The same selection criteria are used in this program
as in the earlier one with the exception of a wider utilization
span for identifying receiving schools.

Obviously, the number of pupils involved in the combined Open Enrollment and Free-Choice Transfer Program is small in relation to the number remaining in *de facto*
segregated schools. Nonetheless, despite the continuing and

ever-increasing concentration of Negro and Puerto Rican pupils in some districts, the program has resulted in an improved ethnic distribution among the city's schools. In 1957-1958, for example, about 51 per cent of the city's elementary schools were "white" (90 per cent or more "white") as compared with only 33 per cent in 1963-1964. At the junior high school level "white" schools decreased from 42 per cent in 1957-1958 to 29 per cent at the latter date.

Table 8 presents, for elementary schools classified according to the status of the school under the Open Enrollment Program, distributions of scores on four indices of the quality of the educational environment afforded by the school. These four indices are: (1) the mean IQ score of sixth-grade pupils in the school on city-wide tests; (2) the mean grade score of sixth-grade pupils in the school on city-wide reading tests; (3) a measure of pupil mobility during the school year expressed as a percentage of the total number of pupils registered in the school on October 1 of that year; (4) the percentage of teachers in the school who are on permanent license.

For each of the indices the scores of the sending schools are found in the sectors of the distribution indicating a lower level of academic performance and perhaps a less favorable educational climate, while the scores of the receiving schools cluster heavily in the end of the distribution showing higher levels of performance.

The uppermost section of the table shows the distribution of mean IQ scores of sixth-grade pupils in schools classified by open-enrollment status. The distribution indicates that almost 99 per cent of the receiving schools had mean IQ scores in the two upper ranges in contrast to less than 6 per cent in the sending schools. In addition, a third of the sending schools had median IQ scores below 85. Among

Table 8—New York City: Selected Variables for Public Elementary Schools in 1961, by Open Enrollment Status, 1961-1963

VARIABLE AND SCORE 1961	Status of School, 1961-1963[a]								PER CENT DISTRIBUTION BY STATUS OF SCHOOL			
	TOTAL No.	%	SENDING No.	%	RECEIVING No.	%	OTHER No.	%	TOTAL	SENDING	RECEIVING	OTHER
IQ[b]												
70-84	58	10.3	37	33.6	0	0	21	6.7	100.0	63.8	0	36.2
85-94	141	25.0	67	60.9	2	1.4	72	23.1	100.0	47.5	1.4	51.1
95-99	64	11.3	5	4.6	9	6.3	50	16.0	100.0	7.8	14.1	78.1
100 and over	301	53.4	1	0.9	131	92.3	169	54.2	100.0	0.3	43.5	56.1
Total	564	100.0	110	100.0	142	100.0	312	100.0	100.0	19.5	25.2	55.3
Reading[c]												
3.5-3.9	3	0.5	2	1.8	0	0	1	0.3	100.0	66.7	0	33.3
4.0-4.9	146	25.9	82	74.5	0	0	64	20.5	100.0	56.2	0	43.8
5.0-5.9	103	18.3	25	22.7	10	7.0	68	21.8	100.0	24.3	9.7	66.0
6.0 and over	312	55.3	1	0.9	132	93.0	179	57.4	100.0	0.3	42.3	57.4
Total	564	100.0	110	100.0	142	100.0	312	100.0	100.0	19.5	25.2	55.3

Pupil Mobility[d]											
75 and over	32	5.7	7	6.4	0	0	25	8.0	100.0	21.9	0	78.1
50-74	152	26.9	57	51.8	11	7.7	84	26.9	100.0	37.5	7.2	55.3
40-49	89	15.8	17	15.4	25	17.6	47	15.1	100.0	19.1	28.1	52.8
Under 40	291	51.6	29	26.4	106	74.6	156	50.0	100.0	10.0	36.4	53.6
Total	564	100.0	110	100.0	142	100.0	312	100.0	100.0	19.5	25.2	55.3
Teachers on Permanent License[e]											
Under 30	18	3.2	9	8.2	1	0.7	8	2.6	100.0	50.0	5.6	44.4
30-49	102	18.1	37	33.6	9	6.3	56	17.9	100.0	36.3	8.8	54.9
50-74	303	53.7	59	53.6	78	54.9	166	53.2	100.0	19.5	25.7	54.8
75 and over	141	25.0	5	4.5	54	38.0	82	26.3	100.0	3.5	38.3	58.2
Total	564	100.0	110	100.0	142	100.0	312	100.0	100.0	19.5	25.2	55.3

a) Recently organized schools are excluded.
b) IQ scores based on city-wide sixth-grade tests. Median IQ for all schools is 99.8.
c) Mean grade score on city-wide sixth-grade tests. Median reading level for all schools is 6.4.
d) Per cent of pupils (excluding first-graders and graduating class) entering or leaving school during school year.
e) Per cent of teachers on permanent license.

Source: Derived from tabulations supplied by the Board of Education, City of New York.

the non-participating schools about 70 per cent had IQ scores of 95 or over and only 7 per cent below 85. Though sending schools comprise less than 20 per cent of the city's elementary schools, they account for more than 40 per cent of the schools with a median IQ score of less than the city "average."

The distribution of mean grade scores on the city-wide sixth-grade reading tests for elementary schools presents a picture very similar to that exhibited by the distribution of mean IQ scores. Thus, more than three-quarters of the sending schools' sixth-graders show an average reading level of less than fifth grade. No receiving school scores as low, and only 20 per cent of the non-participating schools have average reading levels as retarded. Approximately half of all the sending schools have median reading scores two grades less than the average for the city and all but one sending school scored below the city average. Although receiving schools comprise only about one-fourth of the total number of schools, they account for over 40 per cent of schools with mean reading scores of sixth grade and over.

The disparities in pupil mobility scores among the three classes of schools are not quite as marked as those found in the distributions of IQ and reading scores. Nonetheless, whatever effect high rates of pupil turnover during the school year may have on the educational process, it is by no means confined to the sending schools. For the table shows that of the thirty-two schools having the highest mobility scores of 75 per cent and over twenty-five of them, or 78 per cent, are schools which have not been included in the Open Enrollment Program.

From one point of view the distribution of scores on the final index is the most interesting of all. It shows for each school the proportion of teachers on permanent license and is the one factor among those considered that is most directly amenable to administrative control within the school system. In the "average" (median) elementary school in the city, approximately 64 per cent of the teachers are on permanent license. Over 40 per cent of sending schools have less than 50 per cent of their teachers on permanent license as compared with 7 per cent for the receiving schools and 20 per cent among the non-participating schools. Conversely, less than 5 per cent of the sending schools have as many as three-fourths of their teachers on permanent license as compared with approximately 40 per cent and 25 per cent for the receiving and non-participating schools, respectively.

In addition to the transfer programs discussed, the Board of Education is providing other programs and services to pupils in culturally deprived areas of the city. For example, the Higher Horizons program—aimed at the culturally deprived child—seeks to raise pupil aspirations and thereby performance, utilizing a variety of remedial and enrichment techniques. In the school year 1962-1963, there were fifty-two elementary schools included in the Higher Horizons program: 75 per cent were sending schools; no receiving school participates in this program. In the same vein, the after-school study centers that are providing additional tutorial help in reading and mathematics, and offering pupils homework guidance and supervised use of libraries are also located in those areas with the heavy concentrations of sending schools. Furthermore, most sending schools in the Open Enrollment Program are also designated as special service schools. These schools are provided with additional staff and services that other schools do not receive. These include a reduction in the "normal" classroom capacity (from regular 31.5 pupils per class to 28), guidance counselors, other teaching personnel, and other additions to the staff. Thus, the sending schools and other schools having large numbers of the culturally deprived pupils appear to be receiving the bulk of the enrichment programs provided by the Board of Education. In the receiving schools guidance counselors, school-community coordinators, and reading consultants are made available on request. Other efforts include providing extra teaching personnel in the junior high schools and supplementary allotments for textbooks and other instructional materials.

§   Implications and Conclusions

The Open Enrollment Program and the Free-Choice Transfer Program are among the various though not the only or even most recent responses of the Board of Education of New York City to growing concern of citizens about racial and ethnic imbalance in the public schools. Demographic shifts within the city have brought the problem of imbalance into sharp focus. As we have shown, the important demographic trends that influence the school population have been an increase in the number and proportion of Negroes and Puerto Ricans, loss in the white population, continued high residential segregation of Negroes and Puerto Ricans in neighborhoods, and some dispersal of these segregated neighborhoods in Manhattan to other boroughs. In addition, the city's non-public schools have increased their enrollments primarily among white pupils, adding to the already disproportionately large number of Negroes and Puerto Ricans in the public schools.

Many administrative implications arising from operating a transfer program are rather clear-cut. These include establishing criteria of eligibility of both the sending and receiving ends; the consequent necessity for an ethnic census of pupils; the ground rules and procedures for distributing applications and making assignments; the provision of transportation with the constituent problems of routing; and the presentation of the program to the parents and staff at the participating schools.

With respect to the latter, the New York City Board of Education, for example, has recognized that in administering the program, school administrators may be confronted with morale problems on the part of staff and parents. Principals in the sending schools are urged to point out to their staff members that a parent's decision to have his child transferred to another school is an expression of parental desire that his child be educated in a school having greater ethnic variation, perhaps implying by omission that removal of pupils from the school does not necessarily reflect any inadequacy on the part of the school staff. This same rationale is also suggested in discussing the program with parents who prefer not to have their children transferred. A similar approach is implied in "cooling out" parents who request transfer but because of lack of space and the priority system applied in assignments the transfer cannot be effected. Conversely, at the receiving school administrators are confronted with the problem of convincing staff members and resident parents that they are not receiving particularly selected problem children, either behaviorally or academically, and that the presence of "bused-in" children will not negatively affect the caliber and climate of the school.

Our preliminary field inquiries suggest that the morale problem at sending schools is not particularly great either with respect to buttressing an effective self-image on the part of the staff or the adequacy image of the school for disappointed parents. Tentatively at least, it appears that there is a greater problem at the receiving end, though more recently there are indications that principals and staff in conjunction with parent leaders are doing a great deal toward assuring both teachers and resident parents of the absence of negative effects, if not the values of such a program.

The program has not been in operation long enough to appropriately evaluate its effect on the performance levels of the participating students nor its effect in promoting "social intelligence." Preliminary field inquiry does suggest that, though the sorting-out process of voluntary transfers results in the participation of pupils covering a wide range of academic achievement levels and behavioral conformity, there may be a disproportionate representation at the extreme ends—the best and the worst along both the academic and behavioral dimensions—with a scattering along the middle of the scales. Should this prove to be fact rather than impression, problems of evaluation are, of course, compounded. The concern with evaluation, incidentally, is more than one of methodology, for in the long run the invocation of fiscal reasonableness and feasibility must be anticipated, in conjunction with academic and social gains.

The neighborhood school is characteristic of the organization of elementary schools in urban areas. Basic to the notion of the neighborhood school is that for younger children, schools should be easily accessible and along safe-walking routes that avoid traffic hazards. Also built into the idea of the positive value of neighborhood schools is the after-school use of school premises as a neighborhood center for both the children and adults. As a result, the neighborhood school tends to reflect the social, economic, and cultural characteristics of the area it serves. In our major urban centers today and for most Negroes living in these central cities, this means schools located in slum areas and almost exclusively serving children and families from these areas. (At the upper-school levels the neighborhood concept may be less important. These schools can generally serve more extensive geographic areas.)

Many whites and non-whites residing in our neighborhood school districts are recent migrants and they have brought with them the social and educational handicaps of the rural South and Puerto Rico. Added to this problem is that of teacher recruitment into the schools so characterized. First, there is the hesitation of the middle-class teachers to accept a position in a slum school. This is compounded by the built-in limitation of most teacher training that tends to increase the problem of communication barriers across racial, cultural, and economic class lines.

In reviewing the resultant conflict it is obvious that there is broad agreement among the educators and the clients that integrated-school experience is a desirable goal. The real dispute occurs over the definition and selection of the intermediate objectives and the means of obtaining them. In addition, there is the observed tendency of a preoccupation with a numbers distribution at the possible expense of sound educational practice. Thus despite agreement on the ultimate goal, constant redefinition of and agreement on the parameters of that goal is required.

The continued civil rights insistence that school authorities have a responsibility to mitigate the effects of private discrimination which results in residential segregation is understandable. Persistent blindness, however, to the changing population structure in cities is less understandable. The basic condition necessary for integration—defined with respect to numbers and ratios—is the existence of ethnic variations in the pupil population. Growth patterns in the population of racial and ethnic groups in our central cities have removed, in part, this basic condition. Thus demands for integration based upon pupil ratios may never be achieved. It may be hypothesized under these circumstances that priority demands on the Board or Superintendent for achieving such ethnic balance, therefore, will necessarily diminish, if not cease, and may very well provide a basis of disunity among the various civil rights groups.

What are some of the interim and long-run possibilities?

1. *A transfer program.* As our description bears witness, such programs provide escape for relatively small numbers of pupils. In addition to problems with respect to academic-achievement differentials, there are social-class differentials that may in the short-run at least interfere with the program's ultimate aim.

2. *Rezoning of attendance areas.* Changes in existing attendance lines may tend to promote integration though any long-term effect would be contingent upon the growth and trend in the residential location of the population groups involved.

3. *Princeton plan.* This involves the reclassification of schools to handle fewer grades and thus serve larger areas. Occasionally it is possible to promote integration around the edges of segregated neighborhoods by invoking this plan. Its success is contingent upon the size and ethnic heterogeneity of that redefined wider neighborhood. For example, it would not be effective in central Harlem. The plan is also contingent upon the future course of residential succession.

4. *Location of new facilities along boundaries of segregated neighborhoods.* This, too, does not have any promise of long-term effect, given the differential growth patterns of the population groups involved.

If we are able to redefine our goals so that the numbers game does not take precedent over the basic function of public schooling, then perhaps some agreed-upon specific objectives and obtaining means might be achieved. If such redefinition were to be possible, then there would be less disruption between the disputing groups because of disappointments concerning the magic that the client is expecting the Board to be capable of performing. Along these lines the saturation program suggested for New York City warrants close and serious consideration—irrespective of any labels that have already been attached to it (the charge of "separate but equal," the charge of "piecemeal," the charge of "the ploy of compensatory education," and so on). The saturation program has the sincere goal of upgrading the educational quality of schools in those areas that fall below even the minimum requirements—let alone invoking any concept of "excellence." In addition, such a program recognizes that whether or not attempts at transfer and zoning programs are adopted most children remain in their neighborhood schools and that it is these schools—primarily in slum areas—that require special concerted attention from all possible resources.

The New York City saturation program involves special training of teachers for work in target schools; curriculum adjustments so as to make the materials more meaningful to the groups toward which they are oriented; and the priority assignment of counseling services, preventive services, remedial services, and the like. In addition, and perhaps as a by-product, such programs may very well result in upgrading the peer status value of teachers assigned to these schools. This is a necessary step toward the resolution of the recruitment problem.

In the long run, as a result of population changes, insistence that the schooling of Negroes can be satisfactory only if in each schoolroom there are present some white children will necessarily diminish and hopefully cease. As interim measures, transfer programs, rezoning endeavors, and the utilization of integration criteria in the selection of building sites are valuable, though temporary. The real problem is that of providing for these children a sound education, which in turn is contingent upon appropriate curriculum materials and upon the ability to recruit and train teachers for a job that until recently has been foreign to them. Efforts and resources expended along these lines will have perhaps a less immediate but certainly a more permanent long-term effect.

Notes

1. It is recognized that in New York City there is possible conflict within the Board, as well as between the Board and the Superintendent, though the public stance is one of unity. This is in contrast to the well-publicized disunity among Board members in Chicago and Boston. Also recognized is the lack of cohesion among the various parental and civil rights groups. Nonetheless for the immediate purposes the simplified approach may be more instructive than deceptive.

2. Generally, if there is congruence of means and objectives among the various components of a system there would be no conflict.

3. Charles Bidwell, "The School as a Formal Organization," in James G. March, *Handbook of Organizations* (Chicago: Rand, McNally & Company, 1965).

4. James S. Coleman, *The Adolescent Society* (New York: The Free Press, 1961); Wayne Gordon, *The Social System of the High School* (New York: The Free Press, 1957).

5. Board of Education, City of New York, *Plan for Integration,* August, 1963, p. 1.

6. Board of Education, City of New York, News Bureau, Office of Education Information Services and Public Relations, *News Release,* December 28, 1963.

7. Board of Education, City of New York, *Plan for Better Education through Integration*, January 29, 1964.

8. For a description of current pupil population, school organization and programs, staffing procedures, and remedial devices to correct ethnic imbalance, see Eleanor Bernert Sheldon and Raymond A. Glazier, *Pupils and Schools in New York City: A Fact Book* (New York: The Russell Sage Foundation, 1965).

9. U.S. Bureau of the Census, *U.S. Census of Population, 1960, General Population Characteristics, New York*, Final Report PC(1)-34B, Table 20, p. 86; *Census of Population, 1950*, Vol. 2: *Characteristics of the Population*, Part 32, New York, Table 33, p. 84.

Over half of the increase in the non-white population may be attributed to natural increase, suggesting a leveling off of in-migration from the South and an out-migration of some non-white families and individuals to outlying areas.

10. Department of City Planning, New York, *Newsletter*, October, 1962, p. 1.

11. Board of Education, City of New York, *Fifty-eighth Annual Report of the Superintendent of Schools, City of New York, Statistical Section, School Year 1955-1956*, Table 22, p. 59; *Fifty-ninth . . . School Year 1956-1957*, Table 22, p. 64; *Sixtieth . . . School Year 1957-1958*, Table 21, p. 64; *Sixty-first . . . School Year 1958-1959*, Table 21, p. 63; *Sixty-second . . . School Year 1959-1960*, Table 21, p. 60; *Sixty-third . . . School Year 1960-1961*, Table 21, p. 61; *Sixty-fourth . . . School Year 1962-1963*, Table 21, p. 59.

12. U.S. Bureau of the Census, *U.S. Census of Population, 1960, General Social and Economic Characteristics, New York*, Final Report PC(1)-34C, Table 73, p. 266, and Table 77, p. 316.

13. Board of Education, City of New York, *The Open Enrollment Program in the New York City Public Schools: Progress Report, September 1960-September 1963*, p. ii.

14. *Ibid.*, p. ii.

15. *Ibid.*, p. 3.

16. *Ibid.*, p. 3.

17. *Ibid.*, p. 3.

18. *Ibid.*, p. 14.

7

CONTEMPORARY SCHOOL PROBLEMS
AND PUBLIC POLICY

G. Franklin Edwards

Our system of public education is in serious trouble. No group understands this better than the superintendents of our large city schools who must devise remedies for the numerous conditions confronting them. But the problems of our schools are no longer the exclusive, or even major, concern of those who administer the educational system; increasingly they have become the object of public attention and interest. Citizens and educational experts alike have identified areas of malfunctioning in our contemporary schools and have become articulate in their criticisms of the schools' incapacities to solve them. These criticisms are not always grounded in a fundamental understanding of the nature of the problems—their preconditions and precipitating causes. For many critics a species of irrationality exists which makes such understanding irrelevant. It is enough to add that there is, indeed, an observed impatience for finding solutions at the earliest possible time.

Many of the problems faced by our large school systems result from a complex of forces which is broader than the school itself and over which the school system has little or no control. It is true, however, that these problems have served to expose basic weaknesses in our system of public education, particularly at the point of its slowness in developing new educational content, organizational forms, and community linkages. Martin Mayer, an informed analyst of contemporary education, observed recently that "We invented the 20th century. Our schools for complicated reasons got left behind. One of the most important and difficult jobs the United States faces as a nation is to yank its schools into the 20th century." [1]

It is quite evident that many of our school systems have been attempting to meet today's serious problems with an organizational structure and pedagogical orientation better suited to the conditions of a generation or two ago. It is little wonder, then, that schools are severely criticized on many counts and that community conflicts are engendered over educational issues. It is no less surprising that both Federal and state governments and private foundations have assumed more active and powerful roles in the public's efforts to meet the problems of local school systems.

§   The Problems

Increases in Student Population

A heavy contribution to the problems faced by our large-city systems is the substantial increase in the number of children to be educated at the elementary and secondary levels. In the dozen years between 1950 and 1962, the increase in the number of school children at these levels was approximately 16.7 million, with 13.7 million of the increase enrolled in the public schools.[2] The largest proportion of the increase had to be absorbed by public institutions in our large cities. It is hardly necessary to state that this expansion of the school population demanded larger expenditures for school plants, facilities, salaries, and school services if the quality of education was not to be seriously affected. For most local governments and school systems, with serious limitations on their borrowing authority and obvious tax restraints, the accommodations to the expanded pupil loads were made with great difficulty and not without some effects on the quality of educational offerings. It is enough to point out that oversized classes and part-time instruction increased and a larger number of temporary teachers were hired during the period of heavy pupil expansion. The end to this increase in pupil population is not yet in sight. Projections estimate that another 13 million students will enter our elementary and secondary schools by 1975, with 11 million of this number enrolling in public institutions.[3]

The present expansion of the school population results in large part from the high birth rates of the war and postwar years. Demography, however, is not the only explanation of the mushrooming pupil population, which in fact has been moving at varying rates on an upward course for almost three-quarters of a century. Witness, for example, that in 1890 only 3.5 of every 100 young people were graduated from high school. In 1956, 62.3 of every 100 young people were graduated from high school.[4]

Over the past half century education has been viewed increasingly as indispensable for equipping the individual to attain important values of a society which was becoming more highly differentiated—for job qualification, for an adequate income, and for the discharge of his duties as a citizen. External pressures, therefore, were exerted to keep students in school longer—one result of which was an increase in the median educational attainment of the population.

During the postwar years a heavy economic component has been involved in the external pressures to keep students in school. One expression of this involvement is the concern with developing skilled talent to meet increased technical and service needs. As the War on Poverty suggests, there also has been a great effort to avoid the economic, and human, costs of inadequate academic preparation.

This relatively recent attention to the relationship between education and economic well-being is exemplified by the North Carolina Fund, a non-profit, charitable organization incorporated in July, 1963, by a group of North Carolinians, headed by the governor of the state. The fund, which operates with money provided by government and private foundations, has as its objective raising the economic level of citizens of the state through experimental projects conducted within a comprehensive planning framework.[5] These experimental programs will emphasize not only the innovations in education, but also that the inadequate preparation of too large a proportion of the state's population is a primary cause of the state's ranking forty-third among the fifty states in per capita income.[6] The educational programs will be addressed to both adults and persons of school age. The hope for the latter group is that larger numbers of young people will be stimulated to remain in school longer.

Some Consequences of Increases in Enrollment

Increases in the population of elementary and secondary schools have demanded the allocation of more money for education at these levels. Approximately $16 billion, an amount equal to nearly one-sixth of the annual Federal budget, is today spent on public elementary and secondary schools.[7] This expenditure is not sufficiently large, in the judgment of professional educators, to meet existing needs in at least two major categories: teachers and classroom space. These needs will be even greater in the years ahead.

John Gardner of the Carnegie Corporation states that

> During the 1960's the number of classroom teachers will have to expand by almost one-third. To meet both growth and replacement needs, we must recruit at least 200,000 new teachers every year for the next ten years. These are conservative figures. A number of educational leaders have urged a minimum of 50 professionals (teachers, counselors, administrators, etc.) to every 1,000 students. We are far from that today.[8]

The prospect of meeting the demand for additional teachers is poor unless new techniques and incentives are tried. Conant points out that "In 1962, about 143,000 graduates of our colleges and universities were prepared to teach; 55,000 were prospective elementary school teachers, 88,000 were ready for secondary schools." [9] The ratio of elementary teachers to secondary teachers, he notes, is about three to two, while the ratio between those graduated and prepared to teach in 1962 was five to eight in favor of secondary teachers. This would indicate that we are failing to produce a sufficiently high proportion of elementary school teachers. Because many of those prepared to teach do not actually take a job, the annual production of new teachers, Conant estimates, may be nearer 106,000 than 143,000.[10] These deficits cover only certain quantitative aspects of the problem and do not relate to teaching effectiveness and quality of education, which may be, in effect, the most serious aspects of the problem.

As regards classroom space, the U.S. Commissioner of Education, in testimony before a subcommittee of the U.S. Senate Committee on Labor and Public Welfare, noted that a minimum of 121,200 new classrooms is needed, according to official figures reported by the several states.[11] If serious overcrowding is to be reduced, so that elementary schools would average 25 pupils per classroom and secondary schools 20 pupils per classroom, a total of 272,000 additional classrooms would be required.[12] These estimates, however, are based on 1962 enrollment, and thus do not reflect the increases in enrollment that will have to be accommodated during the next decade.

If the needs for additional classrooms reported year after year by the states, which are known to be on the conservative side, are taken as an indication of deficits, the Commissioner concludes, "A serious national problem *does* exist and—educational opportunity and quality *are* being limited." [13]

In view of the reported teacher shortages and the need for additional buildings, it is not surprising that state and Federal contributions to local school systems have increased markedly over the past two decades and must increase even more in the future. New York state revised its state aid to local school districts for educational purposes in 1962, and the Governor's budget message for fiscal 1965 included an additional contribution of $74 million for assistance to local school districts. This constitutes approximately three-quarters of the additional money requested for state aid to local districts for all purposes.[14] In the current fiscal year, *The New York Times* editorializes, $1.3 billion of New York state funds are allotted to education. This sum represents 46 per cent of the entire state budget. More than a billion dollars is state aid to elementary and secondary schools, which represents 42 per cent of local public school costs.[15] In addition, Federal contributions to local school systems for elementary and secondary education increased from $68 million in 1949-1950 to $549 million in 1962-1963.[16]

Non-whites and the Deprived

A large proportion of the population increase of elementary and secondary schools is represented by non-whites, of which Negroes constitute the largest component. The shift of Negroes from the South, which lost approximately 1.5 million non-whites during the 1950-1960 decade, was mainly to the highly industrialized areas of the northeastern, north central, and western states. During that decade the northeastern and north central regions each gained over half a million non-whites through migration, and the western states approximately a third of a million through this means.[17]

The heavy concentration of non-whites in urban communities is indicated by the fact that in 1960 one-third of the members of this group was living in the twenty-five largest cities of the country; 26 per cent were concentrated in the ten largest cities; [18] and seventeen cities had a non-white population in excess of 100,000.[19]

The movement of larger numbers of non-whites into large urban communities occurred alongside a heavy exodus of whites from the central cities to suburban areas. The population of the central cities of the Standard Metropolitan Statistical Areas increased by 4.2 million non-whites during the past decade; 82 per cent of this non-white increase occurred in central cities. In contrast, 83 per cent of the white-population increase of approximately 19 million in the SMSA's occurred in suburban portions of the areas.[20] Because of low average incomes and discriminatory housing, these non-whites were heavily concentrated in densely settled portions of the inner city. In consequence, the schools of the inner city became even more heavily segregated. In Chicago, for example, 91 elementary and high schools are all-white and 56 elementary and secondary schools are all-Negro. Another 281 schools are more than 90 per cent white and 170 schools are more than 90 per cent Negro. Seventy-seven per cent of all public schools in Chicago have 90 per cent or more of one racial group.[21]

The situation is much the same in all large city systems. In New York City, to take another case, at the time the Superintendent of Schools submitted his first report in August, 1963, on plans for racial integration of the schools in that city, 226 of the 578 elementary, junior high, academic, and vocational high schools had 50 per cent or more Negro and Puerto Rican students enrolled, although together these groups constituted less than one-quarter of the total population. In more than one-half of these schools Negroes and Puerto Ricans were 90 per cent or more of the student population.[22]

Two significant points are connected with this development. The increasing housing segregation led to increases in *de facto* segregated school patterns. Despite efforts to relieve the situation in response to the mandate of the 1954 Supreme Court decision and the mounting pressures from community groups, the leverage for effective relief is limited by the housing pattern. The attempt to achieve racial balance in the schools in face of the restrictive housing pattern has led to proposals for rezoning of school districts, transportation of children by buses from their neighborhood schools to schools in other areas, open-enrollment plans, and a number of other devices, all of which have drawn community opposition. This is, indeed, one of the major problems in our large cities, as recent events in New York City and Cleveland, Ohio, demonstrate.

The second point is that the segregated school is identified with inferior education, and parents of children attending such schools are insisting that present inequalities be corrected. These schools, particularly those in the worst slums, are inferior for a number of reasons and are in need of considerable improvement, if not complete overhaul, a matter to be discussed later in this paper.

The high visibility of these schools with their inferior physical facilities, their highly concentrated ethnic populations, and their disproportionate rates of academic failures, dropouts, and delinquency, has brought them forcibly to the attention of the public. We have always had such schools, but the reaction to them today is more vigorous and sharply critical than at any other time. The consciousness of their existence and their products comes at a time when minority-group aspirations for a more equitable share of community benefits have risen sharply; and these groups insist that the education offered their children be improved.

The broader public has had ample reason to become concerned about the status of these slum schools. Their dysfunctional nature is apparent in a period when the social and occupational characteristics of the country have changed markedly. The products of these schools are almost always found in unskilled jobs when unskilled jobs are not so numerous as before. As a group they are not prepared to enter the expanding areas of technical and clerical services. Our manpower-retraining experiences have demonstrated that many of the products of these schools, particularly those who drop out before finishing high school, are unable, as a result of their low literacy level, to take advantage of the opportunities offered for skill development.

The recent report of the President's Task Force on Manpower Conservation increases our knowledge of the inability of young men with inadequate education to qualify for useful lives. A study of a nationwide sample of twenty-five hundred men between the ages of twenty and twenty-four who failed to pass the selective service examination revealed that

> Only 69 per cent of the group had jobs. Their rate of unemployment was 28 per cent—four times greater than for all young men in the 20-24 age group. In addition, 5 per cent were out of work and were not looking for work at the time of the survey. The unemployment rate of non-whites was somewhat higher than for whites—29 per cent as compared with 26 per cent.[23]

The report also indicates that four out of five rejectees were school dropouts. About half left school before age seventeen. Only 75 per cent had finished grade school, as compared with 95 per cent of all men in their age group, and only 20 per cent had completed high school. In general, the median years of schooling for rejectees was approximately one-quarter less than that for the total male population of comparable age.[24]

§   Internal and External Pressures Suggesting the Need for Reform

The present and projected student-population increase stress the need for new means of financing our school systems if the latter are to cope with the problems they experience. In the past, without proper financing, accommodation has been made through a system of inequalities, with some areas having better schools than others. Sexton's study [25] of a large-city school system develops the inequalities in achievement which result from many factors, one of which is the cultural background and general preparation of the child. No one would argue that education received in the worst areas of our cities is of the same quality as that offered in schools in the higher economic areas; a gradient, in fact, exists on all of the factors which enter into the production of educational quality.

So enormous have been the burdens facing the managers of our school systems that the schools themselves have generated little innovation. Where innovations have been introduced, they generally have been directed to the better schools—introduction of honors programs, for example. Unfortunately, institutional behavior is characterized by conservatism rather than by innovation.

In systems where a track program has been introduced, this device has been advanced as educationally sound and meeting the needs of the various subgroups of the school population. Homogeneous groupings according to ability, it is contended, permit the student to advance according to his ability. The argument is logical, although some contend that the real problem is to make heterogeneous ability groupings work.[26] These people argue that the track program works a hardship on pupils in the lower tracks by reinforcing their sense of being different and contributes to the development of low self-esteem.

Whatever the merits of the respective arguments, and merit appears inherent in each, clearly the limited funds available to schools have not permitted an attack on the problems of pupils in the lower tracks. On balance, it would appear that pedagogical problems of low-income pupils are more serious and should be given a disproportionately greater share of the available resources. This means the best available teachers, facilities, teaching technologies, and money for experimentation. This, in fact, has not been the case. The parents of students in the lower tracks are not so sensitive to what is occurring in the schools as are the parents of those in the honors' and college-preparatory courses. They do not question either students or teachers in the same manner as do parents of students in the upper tracks.

The highly organized parent-teacher associations in the middle-and upper-class neighborhoods keep the teachers and superintendents informed of family environments of children of these classes. But there is little intimate understanding of the conditions under which most children in the lower tracks live. In those instances where school systems are bold enough to depart from their insularity to investigate the out-of-school problems of these children, under the legitimacy of looking into the reasons for poor school performance, the data obtained are not systematically collected and are seldom, if ever, used to develop corrective programs.

One study of children who failed both the Metropolitan Readiness Test and, later, the first grade revealed that approximately three-fourths of the group had low hemoglobin levels (below 12 grams), and one-third had unsatisfactory levels (below 11 grams). Other physical defects revealed included central nervous system pathologies, visual problems, hearing loss, congenital defects, and allergies. Family income placed the majority of their parents at or near the poverty level. Poor living accommodations, broken families, and family dependency were characteristic. Already the children had developed numerous psychological symptoms: enuresis, drooling, hyperactivity, nail biting, speech difficulties, etc.[27]

The study was an action-research program with experimental and control groups and was conducted over a period of approximately two years. The results were not salutary, owing to the limited in-put vis-à-vis the seriousness of the problems the children experienced. They did, however, suggest that changes were possible.

The most important reason for mentioning this study is that it reveals something about the organizational readiness, or lack of it, of school systems to meet the problems of children of the type studied. Many recommendations were made to the superintendent and the school board for correcting the conditions uncovered. These suggested additional responsibilities by the school for special programs, including a separate experimental school for students with similar problems. It also was recommended that other community agencies become involved with the school system in a team effort to meet the needs of these children and thereby facilitate their learning and adjustment. Though the recommendations were made more than two years ago, nothing has been done to implement them. Pupils of this type continue to be taught by conventional methods, although it is evident that they are unable to profit from them. As the process continues, the inevitable consequence is school failure and negative self-concepts, with the understandable prediction that many children will leave school as soon as possible.

Studies of the type mentioned above reveal the inadequacy of the conventional school organization to meet the problems of what is often referred to as the lower 30 per cent of the pupil population. The teachers are drawn mainly from middle-class backgrounds and have neither the professional training or other experience to cope with problems of lower-class youngsters. Even if they had, the demands of conventional programs preclude their giving the necessary time to exploring new curriculum materials and pedagogical methods. One might bring into question the ability of the entire range of school services to meet the pressing problems of the group under discussion. This would apply particularly to school counselors and school health personnel. As for research bureaus, one need only state that extremely able people are often hired, only to be put to work on standard test and measurement problems.

Any effective program for remedying the problems of urban school systems will call for vast amounts of money, and the need for new money is often advanced as the basic reason for the failure of the schools to develop viable experimental programs. I submit that even more fundamental for any program for coping with the problems encountered by educational institutions in urban areas is an understanding of the nature of the problems and a commitment to do something about them. These fundamentals have not usually been present, and when they have the bureaucratic structure of our school systems has often kept them from being translated into meaningful programs.

The external forces posing problems for the school system have already been mentioned and are repeated only to emphasize the need for new relationships within the school and between the school and other community agencies. If a more even racial balance is desirable in our schools, then segregated housing must be eliminated. Temporary relief may be secured by carefully planning new school locations, especially in marginal areas, and by pairing schools, the Princeton Plan, and other piecemeal measures. But school authorities must look toward the moderation of segregation and discrimination in housing in the general community. Much precious time is spent trying to develop more evenly balanced racial mixes in the schools. I do not believe that this is unimportant; I argue only that segregated housing as a community pattern places an undue burden on the schools, because they are forced to become predominantly white or predominantly Negro. In the interest of doing something about this problem, superintendents, school-board members, and parent-teacher associations should support the efforts of local governments and community groups whose objective is the elimination of housing segregation.

Many problems which low-income pupils bring into the schools are not the primary responsibility of the schools, but they must be dealt with if effective learning is to occur. The school is in a good position to identify the pupils who are in trouble, but at present it is not staffed to handle the underlying contributing conditions. So, the school must join other community welfare agencies in a team effort to work on these problems. Such a cooperative relationship is not easy to fashion in terms of existing vested interests in agency prerogatives.

In concluding this section, it is sufficient to point out that our schools appear to operate quite well with our middle- and upper-class populations, although Admiral Rickover and others may not think so.[28] Certainly there is room for improvement of instruction and, as the work of the Physical Science Survey Committee demonstrates, much is to be gained from further study of curriculum changes and learning processes.

A high, if not the highest, priority problem of the public schools today is to find techniques for educating effectively the large segment of the school population designated as culturally deprived. The problem is posed by the inability of our conventional school organization and orientation to meet the needs of these youngsters, on the one hand, and by the changing character of the social and economic life of or urban communities, on the other.

The problem cannot be met unless our present concepts

and techniques are radically reorganized. New experimental methods must be explored. The problem is so massive that local communities do not have the necessary money or talent to make the desired impact.

§ Further Implications for Public Policy

Our present knowledge of what should be done to improve the education of the disadvantaged is so inadequate that nothing short of large-scale experimental programs is indicated. Therefore, the services of various elements of the public must be enlisted, including the universities, private foundations, labor organizations, the business community, and government. In some manner the entire country is affected by the present uneven quality of education: dependency and antisocial conduct increase as larger numbers of citizens become unable to cope with their environment.

After the preceding discussion, it is not difficult to discern why the approach to the problem must be massive: it must be massive in order to create either radical modification of existing methods or completely new structures, or both. One suggested approach is a number of experimental or model schools, some of which would be operated apart from existing school systems, so that those in charge would have the necessary freedom and control to test their ideas.[29]

Such schools would take into account many of the deficiencies of conventional programs. They would build upon the fact that the problems of these children begin early and therefore enrichment programs should begin before the children enter school. These programs would involve not only the children but their parents as well, so that adult education would be carried alongside training of the youngsters. Preparation of these pupils for reading, listening, and the manipulation of objects would be stressed. Such training may go on for a number of years, depending upon what is necessary.[30]

One important aspect of such a program is that it would depart from conventional grading systems during the early period. Essentially, the schools will be ungraded. They would have the advantage, moreover, of the best in our educational technology—reading machines, television, programmed instruction. Team teaching would be used where indicated.

One intriguing possibility of such schools is that they would attract the best personnel—scholars in education and the behavioral sciences who have a fundamental interest in learning more of the cognitive styles and potentials of the school population. There is, indeed, a growing number of professional persons who have begun in limited ways to test their ideas regarding the learning problems of the under-privileged.[31] They doubtless would welcome the opportunity to participate in such programs. But one of the real strategies would be to broaden the number of persons with intimate knowledge of learning theory as applied to this population, so that these model schools should serve as training grounds for practice teachers.

An attractive possibility which such schools offer is the development of new curriculum materials. A significant part of the problem of underprivileged children in conventional school settings is that the materials are foreign to their experiences and fail to capture their interests.

These experimental or model schools may be operated on many levels—elementary, junior high, and senior high. They may involve work-study programs and other aspects of vocational education. Hopefully, some of these programs will carry forward an educational sequence from the preschool level through high school. The large expenditure of time and money will not be disproportionately costly for what might be learned from such programs.

The growing conviction that model schools must be set up does not eliminate the possibility of attacking educational problems in less novel ways, that is, through modification of existing arrangements. Any such undertaking, however, has certain minimum conditions which must be met. In the first instance, some liaison must be established on a continuing basis between the school and the families of the pupils. The establishment of a new occupational status, the school-community agent, has been suggested. The duty of persons filling this role would be to serve as a liaison between school and family by informing teachers of the home conditions of pupils, and by working with parents on the school problems of their children. The school-community agent, moreover, would assist families with many problems by directing them to the appropriate community agencies.

If the problems are to be remedied within the existing framework, teachers must have greater latitude to experiment with curriculum materials. The teachers selected must be among the most able, and a system of incentives must be developed. The incentives should include higher salaries, but consideration should be given also to reduction in class schedules and, in general, to a recognition of the importance of the undertaking. At present our more able teachers have not been heavily involved in teaching the deprived, largely because they have not remained on the staffs of schools in slum and blighted areas. As they gain experience and develop skills, the able teachers usually request transfers. The mobility of teachers in slum schools is too well known to warrant further comment. The value placed upon the importance of the task will determine whether able teachers will be attracted to it.

School superintendents and administrators will play a crucial role in determining the success or failure of any program directed to the problem within the school system. Their cooperation in defining the task as important is indispensable to the success of the venture. In addition to providing the school-community agents and incentives for the best teachers, they must make available the necessary physical materials with which teachers must work. Too often in the past the slum and blighted area schools have not fared well in the distribution of school resources. Finally, the superintendents and other administrators must be committed to taking what is learned and incorporating it into the school's instructional program.

One is impressed with the fact that so much of the little we know about the problem discussed has come from individual investigators and agencies not formally connected with the public schools. The philanthropic foundations have played a significant role by supporting research which bears upon the problem. The Ford Foundation Gray Areas projects, which ally the schools with other community agencies in a coordinated attack upon the problems of the underprivileged, demonstrate valuable approaches. Other major foundations are also prepared to offer substantial support to the model or experimental school idea.

One is impressed also with the significant role of the Federal government in providing ideas and money with which to attack the problem. The National Science Foundation, the National Institutes of Health, The U.S. Office of Education, The President's Committee on Juvenile Delinquency and Youth Crime, and the Office of Science and

Technology of the Executive Department have made valuable contributions both by generating interest in the significance of educational problems and by using their resources in supporting research and special programs. The workshops and conferences on educational problems which these agencies have either conducted themselves or otherwise supported are especially deserving of mention. In recent years these agencies have shown an increasing willingness to cooperate with one another in sponsoring research and special programs. Beyond this is the emerging cooperative relationship between agencies of the Federal and state governments and the private foundations.

These cooperative patterns signify that a consensus is emerging regarding the importance of the problems of education and feasible approaches to their solution. There is a growing awareness in all quarters that something must be done to conserve manpower which is likely to be wasted under conventional programs. To neglect the problem is too costly both for the nation and for the deprived individuals. It would appear that in their readiness to act on the fundamental problems of the schools, representatives of the Federal government and the foundations are ahead of the schoolmen. The latter cannot afford to be left too far behind.

I conclude this paper with the observation that since the public school system was established in the nineteenth century, an education has been regarded as an important need of all individuals in a democratic society: it equips them to qualify for opportunities and for upward mobility and permits the discharge of their duties as citizens. Although the elementary and secondary levels of our school systems are rooted in the local community, as the educational process becomes more complex the Federal and state governments become more intimately involved. Variations have been observed in the quality of education between local school districts within states and between states, but until recently these differences were not regarded as a serious threat to the society. In the complex society of today, with increased spatial mobility and more demanding requirements for job qualifications, the observed inequalities within and between school systems must be viewed with concern. Failure to take aggressive action to eliminate the differences in educational quality is costly to the nation and is tantamount to default by those in position to offer assistance. It is for these reasons that our schools today become of greater concern as matters of public policy.

Notes

1. Martin Mayer, "Last Chance for Our Schools," *The Saturday Evening Post* (September 14, 1963), p. 24.

2. *Fall Enrollment in Grades K-8 and 9-12 of Regular Public and Non-public Day Schools in 50 States and the District of Columbia: 1949-1975*, (Division of Educational Statistics, Office of Education, U.S. Department of Health, Education, and Welfare, 1963).

3. *Loc. cit.*

4. U.S. Bureau of the Census, *Historical Statistics of the United States: Colonial Times to 1957* (2nd printing; Washington, D.C. Government Printing Office, 1961), Series H-223, p. 207.

5. *The North Carolina Fund: Programs and Policies* (Durham, N.C.: The North Carolina Fund, November 25, 1963), pp. 5-7.

6. *Ibid.*, p. 9.

7. U.S. Bureau of the Census, *Statistical Abstract of the United States* (84th ed.; Washington, D.C., 1963), Table 144, p. 115.

8. John W. Gardner, "National Goals in Education," *Goals for Americans* (Report of the President's Commission on National Goals (New York: Spectrum Book S-AA-3, 1960), p. 82.

9. James B. Conant, "Supply and Demand of Teachers," *The*

Education of American Teachers (New York: McGraw-Hill Book Company, Inc., 1963), Appendix D, p. 229.

10. *Loc. cit.*

11. From Statement by Francis Keppel, Commissioner of Education, Department of Health, Education, and Welfare, before the Subcommittee on Education of the Committee on Labor and Public Welfare U.S. Senate, Tuesday, June 25, 1963, p. 37.

12. *Ibid.*, p. 38.

13. *Ibid.*, p. 39.

14. *The New York Times,* January 23, 1964, p. 22.

15. *The New York Times,* October 9, 1964, p. 36.

16. Ida C. Merriam, "Social Welfare Expenditures, 1962-1963," *Social Security Bulletin,* XXVI (November, 1963), Table 8, p. 12.

17. *Our Nonwhite Population and Its Housing: The Changes Between 1950 and 1960* (Washington, D.C.: Office of the Administrator, Housing and Home Finance Agency, April, 1963), Table 1A.

18. *Ibid.*, Table 6.

19. *Ibid.*, Table 7.

20. *Ibid.*, Table 4A.

21. *The Chicago Sun-Times,* October 24, 1963.

22. Board of Education, City of New York, *Plan for Integration,* August 23, 1963.

23. *One-third of a Nation: A Report on Young Men Found Unqualified for Military Service,* Report of the President's Task Force on Manpower Conservation (Washington, D.C., January 1, 1964), p. 15.

24. *Ibid.*, p. 16.

25. Patricia Sexton, *Education and Income* (New York: The Viking Press, 1961).

26. Martin Deutsch, "Dimensions of the School's Role in the Problems of Integration," in Gordon J. Klopf and Israel A. Laster (eds.), *Integrating the Urban School* (New York: Teachers College, Columbia University, 1963), pp. 37-38.

27. *An Action-Research Project for Identifying and Modifying Problems That Affect the Mental Health of Certain First-Grade Pupils and the Mental Health of Their Classrooms* (Department of Pupil Appraisals, Study and Attendance, Public Schools of the District of Columbia, 1962).

28. H. G. Rickover, *American Education: A National Failure* (New York: E. P. Dutton & Co., Inc., 1963).

29. The model-school idea is discussed in *Innovation and Experiment in Education,* Progress Report of the Panel on Educational Research and Development (The President's Science Advisory Committee, Executive Office Building, Washington, D.C.).

30. See, for example, the papers from the Arden House Conference on Preschool Enrichment, *The Merrill-Palmer Quarterly,* X, No. 3 (July, 1964).

31. See the contributions of educators and behavioral scientists to the following volumes: A. Harry Passow (ed.), *Education in Depressed Areas* (New York: Bureau of Publications, Teachers College, Columbia University, 1963); and the special issue of *The Journal of Negro Education,* XXXIII, No. 3 (Summer, 1964) entitled, "Educational Planning for Socially Disadvantaged Children and Youth."

Index

§ Name Index

Abramson, David A., 151
Allen, Ruth J., 151
Argyris, Chris, 108
Austin, Mary, 127, 151

Barnhart, Clarence L., 151
Baumann, Mayvis L., 151
Berelson, Bernard, 98
Berg, Marcia E., 151
Bidwell, Charles, 188
Blau, Peter, 65, 97
Blessington, Mary A., 151
Bloomfield, Leonard, 151
Board of Education, New York City,
189, 212
Brameld, Theodore, 124-125
Brauner, Charles J., 151
Bruns, Hobert W., 151
Burns, Eugene H., 30, 45
Byerly, Carl L., vii

Cartwright, Dorwin, 96
Cicourel, Aaron V., 31, 45
Class, Norris E., 45
Cohen, Albert 99
Cohen, R. A., 97
Cohen, S. Allen, 7
Coleman, James S., 154-155, 188
Conant, James B., 195, 211
Crawford, P. L., 98
Cunningham, William J., vii

Davis, F. James, 98
Dearing, Bruce, 151
Deutsch, Martin, 212
Dewey, John, 121, 124, 151
Dienstein, William, 22, 33, 44-45
Dodge, Donald G., 43
Dumpson, J. R., 98

Eckstrom, Ruth B., 151-152
Edwards, G. Franklin, 7, 13
Empey, La Mar, 38, 46, 98
Englund, Frederick W., 46
Esselstyn, T. C., 29, 44

Gardner, John W., 195, 211
Gaudet, Hazel, 98
Genua, Florence P., 152
Gladwin, Thomas, 33, 46
Gordon, Wayne, 155
Gouldner, Alvin, 24, 28, 30, 34, 41,
44-45, 47
Grant, Douglas, 46
Greenblatt, Milton, 96-97
Gross, Neal, 19, 99, 108

Hansen Carl, vii
Hare, A. Paul, 108
Harris, Anna S., 136, 152
Hilgard, Ernest R., 152
Hopkins, Mark, 129
Horowitz, David A., vii

Hylton, Lydia F., 98
Hyman, Herbert H., 98
Hypps, Irene C., vii

Janowitz, Morris, viii, 97
Jarvie, Lawrence L., vii
Jefferson, Thomas, 121

Kahn, Robert, 108
Kallen, Horace M., 152
Kat, Daniel, 98
Katz, Elihu, 98
Kenney, John P., 44
Keppel, Francis, 212
Kitsuse, John, 31, 45
Kobrin, Solomon, 98

Landers, Jacob, vii
Larson, William R., 44
Lazarsfeld, Paul, 98
Lebeaux, Charles N., 97
Lefever, D. Welty, 45
Levinson, Daniel J., 96
Likert, Rensis, 108
Lippitt, Ronald, 15, 18, 96
Litwak, Eugene, 12, 96-98
Longstreth, Langdon E., 45

McEachern, A. W., 19, 44
Malamud, D. I., 98
Mann, Floyd, 108
Mann, Horace, 121
Marburger, Carl L., vii, 49
March, James G., 96-97
Mason, Ward S., 19
Mayer, Martin, 192, 211
Merriam, Ida C., 212
Meyer, Henry, 12, 96
Miller, S. M., 35, 46
Miller, Walter B., 47, 99
Mobilization for Youth, New York
    City, 126, 138
Murphy, Helen, 152

Nelson, E. K., 6-7, 43-44, 46-47
New York City Youth Board, 95
New York *Times,* 152

Ohlin, Lloyd E., 44, 99
Olson, Arthur V., 152

Palmer, Ted, 44
Pappenfort, Donnel, M., 44
Parsons, Talcott, 19, 24, 51, 95
Passow, A. Harry, 213
Paulson, Blanche B., vii
Petersen, William, 98
Pfittner, John, 25-26, 42, 44, 47
Piven, Herman, 44
President's Committee on Juvenile
    Delinquency and Youth Crime,
    viii, 210

Rabow, Jerome, 46, 98
Rasschaert, William, 49
Reiss, Albert J., Jr., 99, 108
Rice, Roger E., 45
Rickover, H. G., 205, 213

Saunders, Alta M., 152
Schmuck, Richard A., 106, 120
Scott, Richard W., 97
Sexton, Patricia, 200, 212
Shanley, Fred J., 45
Sheatsley, Paul, 98
Sheldon, Eleanor Bernert, 9
Shils, Edward A., 97
Shreve, John W., vii
Sigurdson, Herbert R., 43
Simon, Herbert A., 96-97
Smith, Jr., William T., vii

Theodorson, George A., 95
Thompson, James D., 97
Trace, Arthur S., 128, 152

Van Egmond, Elmer E., 106, 120

Vinter, Robert, viii, 50, 98
Von Mehring, Otto, 96

Walcutt, Charles C., 128, 152
Watson, Goodwin, 138, 152
Weber, Max, 51 54-55 66, 68, 96-97
Weinswig, S. Edward, 152
White, Ralph A., 96
Wilensky, Harold W., 97
Williams, Frederick, vii

Williams, Richard, 96
Wormell, Helen E., 106, 120
Wylie, Laurence, 36, 46

Youth Studies Center, University of
Southern California, 22, 28, 31-32,
35-36, 47

Zander, Alvin, 96

§ Subject Index

Accountability, civic, 40
Achievement
    academic, 180-181, 188, 199
    orientation, 106
Action programs, 99, 109-110, 119,
    122, 202-203, 206
Adaptation, 11
Administration, 66, 68, 71, 153
Administrators, 42, 153 (see also
    School, administrators)
Adolescence, 21
    socialization of, 31
Adolescent deviance (see Youth, de-
    viance)
Adolescent peer group (see Youth,
    organization)
Authority
    delegation of, 12, 84-88
    formal organization of, 22, 24,
        37, 62, 84-85, 87-88
    informal organization of, 105
Automation, 121, 156

Bureaucracy, forms of, 1, 50, 52-53,
    55, 58, 66, 69, 77, 94

Civil rights, 133, 156, 185
Classroom, social organization of,
    103, 105-107, 113-114
Communication, 106, 109-110, 185
Community institutions, 23, 38

Community leaders, 100-103, 111,
    120
    economic, 101-102
    educational, 101-102
    religious, 101-102
    therapeutic, 101-102
Community, organization of, 27, 38,
    51-52, 99, 102
Community, school relations (see
    School, community relations)
Conformity—nonconformity, 38, 101
Cooperation, 40
    organizational, 42
Culturally deprived youth, 125-126,
    188, 201, 205
Curriculum, 15-17, 32, 107, 109,
    188, 201, 207-208

Decision making, 58, 122
Delinquency, 31, 102, 112, 121, 126,
    129
    prevention, 36-37, 120
Delinquent peer groups (gangs),
    22, 26-27, 31, 38-39, 67, 79
Demonstration projects, 40
Desegregation, 8-10, 156
Detached workers, 78-79, 87-90
Deviant behavior (see Youth, devi-
    ance)
Diffusion, organization for, 114
Dropouts, 9-11, 200

Education
    goals of, 24, 51, 107, 109, 122-
        123, 126, 128, 150, 154, 156
    quality of, 124, 129-151, 199
Educators (see School, professionals)
Enrichment programs, 206
Enrollment programs
    free-choice transfer, 176, 182,
        186, 188
    open, 172-177, 181-182
    Princeton plan, 186, 204
    rezoning, 186
Enrollment, school, 126, 167-171,
    173-174, 196-198
Ethnic balance in schools, 156, 163-
    171, 197-199

Families and schools, 52-53, 112,
    114
Family, 31, 126
Feedback in organizations, 75, 112,
    114

Group dynamics techniques, 32

Higher horizons program, New York
    City, 181

Influentials (see Community leaders)
Innovation, 8, 15-18, 103, 111, 114,
    119-120
    structural, 41, 111, 114, 201
Institutional spheres (systems), 24-
    25
Integration, 40, 42
    plans, 153-188
Intelligence quotient (I.Q.), 105,
    131, 177-180

Job training, 194, 199-200

Law enforcement, 24-25, 102
Leaders (see Community leaders)

Leadership, 105-106
Learning, 107, 124-126, 128-129
    content of, 129, 132, 137
    programmed, 143-144

Mass media, 87-88
Mechanisms of organizational link-
    age, 50, 56, 68, 70, 73, 95
Motivation to learn, 70, 108, 113,
    142-143

Neighborhood
    organization, 106
    schools, 7, 184-185
New York City, 9-10
Norms, 25, 32, 36, 39

Opinion leaders, 79-80, 87-88
Organization
    environment transactions, 10
    of tasks, 66, 68
Organizational
    adaptation, 13, 15, 19
    autonomy, 5-7, 83-95
    disparity, 36-41
    efficiency (effectiveness), 59,
        62, 64-65, 68-69
    goals, 1, 22-23, 66
    linkage, 49-50 (see also School,
        linkage)
    policy, 68
    strategies and tactics, 25
Organizations
    dysfunctions of, 22, 24, 41, 64
    functions of, 23-24

Parent-school relationships, 51, 102,
    106, 109, 118, 183-184
Parent-teacher organizations, 13, 81-
    82, 91, 102
Peer culture (see Youth, culture)
Peer organization (see Youth, organ-
    ization)

Planning, educational (see School, planning)

Police, 21-22, 24-26, 30-31, 33-34, 38, 40, 42

Population
changes in, 158, 185, 192-193
composition of, 160-167
problems, 121

Pressure groups, 3, 13, 155

Primary groups, 83 (see also Delinquent peer groups, Family, and Youth, organization)

Probation, 22, 25, 27-30, 33, 38, 40, 42
officers, 24, 28

Professional socialization agents, 100, 108

Provo experiment, 38-39

Psychotherapy, 29, 65, 67

Pupils, 61, 109, 203

Pupil transfer, 16-17

Reading, 122-123, 127-129, 137-138, 206
readiness, 135-136, 202
tests, 131, 180-181

Reciprocity, 24, 28, 40, 42-43

Rehabilitation, 24, 102, 112

Remedial
programs, 32
reading, 138

Rewards in schools, 143

Role playing, 115

Sanctions, 32

School
administrators, 2, 6-7, 12-13, 61, 109-110, 123, 128, 157, 183
boards, 3, 10, 13, 104, 154, 157, 180
community relations, 12, 50-52, 54, 61, 76, 78, 80, 82, 86-87, 92-94, 122, 182, 208-209
environment, 3-4, 11
linkage, 50, 53, 89-95
planning, 8-10, 107
principals, 12-13, 53, 57-58, 61, 79, 127
professionals, 2-3, 5, 12, 15, 18, 80-81, 121, 123-125, 128, 136, 150, 155
roles, 57

Schools
administrative organization of, v, 13, 15, 35, 123, 155, 182
administrative styles of, 12, 50, 53-61, 69, 78, 89, 91, 93-94
—autocratic, 57-60, 69, 73
—human relations, 55, 58-60, 69, 71-73, 89-94
—laissez-faire, 58-60, 69, 73
—nepotistic, 59-60, 68-69, 73, 92
—paternalistic, 57-60, 69, 73
—professional, 56, 59-60, 69, 71-73, 89, 91-93
—rationalistic, 55, 57-60, 69, 71-73, 89-94
attitudes toward, 38
bureaucratic organization of, 54, 65
changes in, 1-2
collegial authority, 63-64
decision making in, 61-64, 122, 153
effects of, 31
efficiency and effectiveness of, 69-70, 77, 109-110, 157
formal organization of, 5-6, 8, 49, 59, 154-155, 157, 192
goals of, 1-2, 7, 9, 18, 32, 34, 58-59, 61, 70-71, 78, 102, 122, 154-155, 185, 187
hierarchical organization of, 16, 54, 61, 63, 64, 89
ideology of, 33

problems of, 13-14, 23, 154, 191-192
task organization in, 62, 65, 70
Segregation, 8-9
residential, 9, 121, 198, 204
school, 155, 173, 198-199, 204
Settlement house, 80-81, 87-88, 90
Social
distance, 51-53, 76-77, 90, 93-94
problems, 24, 37
Socialization, 71-72, 100, 103, 113, 154
community, 100, 113
—functions of, 100
—professional, 102-103
Subsystems, 24, 39-40
Superintendent of schools, 127, 154, 157, 191, 198, 209

Teacher-pupil relationships, 105-106, 108, 115-117
Teachers, 12, 17, 79, 104, 113-114, 119, 123-128, 180-181, 203
Teaching methods, 70-71, 109, 114, 122-123, 128-131, 139-140, 155
Therapeutic agents, 101
Training, in-service, 104, 113, 120

Values, student, 107, 112
Voluntary associations, 81-82, 87-88

Youth, 5, 101-104, 122
culture, 36, 104, 110
deviance, 21-23, 25, 42, 101-102
organization, 18, 38-39, 104-107, 118
programs, 39, 41, 104, 109